Multibank Holding Company Performance

Research for Business Decisions, No. 52

Gunter Dufey, Series Editor

Professor of International Business and Finance
The University of Michigan

Other Titles in This Series

Multibank Holding Company Performance

by
Ronald L. Schillereff

UMI RESEARCH PRESS
Ann Arbor, Michigan

Produced and distributed by
UMI Research Press
an imprint of
University Microfilms International
Ann Arbor, Michigan 48106

Library of Congress Cataloging in Publication Data

Schillereff, Ronald L. (Ronald Leroy)
Multibank holding company performance.

(Research for business decisions ; no. 52)
Revision of thesis (D.B.A.)–University of Colorado at
Boulder, 1982.
Bibliography: p.
Includes index.
1. Bank holding companies–United States–Evaluation.
2. Banks and banking–United States–Evaluation.   I. Title.
II. Series.
HG2567.S34 1982   332.1'6   82-8583
ISBN 0-8357-1348-2   AACR2

9-28-83
kmm

Contents

Public Policy Implications
Recommendations for Further Research

Figures

Tables

1

An Introduction to the Issues

Statement of the Problem

Banking structure in the United States is currently in a state of evolution. In our society the structure of banking is determined by several economic and noneconomic factors. Two basic factors which affect this structure are the fundamental economic and legal forces in our banking system. In any marketplace the demand for a final product influences the number of sellers. Consequently, within the banking industry the demand for banking services affects the number of banks and their relative size. Complementing this economic demand are various governmental regulations and restrictions which have also had a significant impact on the number and the size of the commercial banks in our society.

A major development in our banking structure which has occurred over the past two decades has been the growth and development of bank holding companies which own or control directly or indirectly one or more banks. The two basic types of bank holding companies which exist are the multibank holding company (MBHC) and the one-bank holding company (OBHC). As these bank holding companies have grown and matured, various research interests relative to this form of banking organization and the changes in the banking structures and practices that have accompanied it have expanded.

One of the more contemporary issues is whether or not the creation and growth of the MBHCs affect a bank's subsequent performance. Stated more precisely, the issue is twofold: Do banks acquired by MBHCs perform any differently from independent banks, and if they do, what factors account for these differences in bank performance or behavior? These questions are of special concern to bank regulators and state and national legislators charged with formulating public policy. The Board of Governors of the Federal Reserve System, in particular, has a deep interest in this question because it has the responsibility of ruling on whether or not a particular bank acquisition should be permitted.

The specific purpose of this study is to investigate empirically how well MBHC affiliate banks perform relative to their local independent bank counterparts. The study is national in scope, yet it examines the individual performance of selected commercial banks. It analyzes the reported financial data of these banks. The major emphasis is on the relative performance of commercial banks acquired by multibank holding companies.[1] This study is interested in determining whether holding company affiliate banks perform any differently, once they have been acquired, from independent banks of comparable size operating under similar market conditions.

A comparison of selected measures of performance of the banking affiliates of MBHCs with nonaffiliated, or independent, banks competing in the same local markets for selected time periods will be conducted. The results of this empirical investigation are examined to determine if there are any public policy implications for our appropriate bank regulators, for Congress, and for our state legislatures. Specifically, both the near and longer term policies of the Federal Reserve Board toward MBHC formation and expansion will be reviewed in light of those factors which account for any performance differences highlighted in this study.

Importance of the Study

The issue of relative performance differences between holding company affiliate banks and independent banks has significant implications for the Federal Reserve Board, individual commercial bank managements, bank customers, and the U.S. banking system as a whole. Both macroeconomic and microeconomic issues are involved. The parties ultimately affected by MBHCs range from individual bank officers and directors to individual bank customers. This study examines how these parties are ultimately affected by subsequent structural changes to the U.S. banking system.

To individual bank shareholders, owning equity in a bank holding company represents a diversified risk in the fast growing field of banking and closely related financial activities. If bank holding companies continue to grow and expand, one result might be a counter-cyclical effect on corporate earnings. For example, in years where the earnings of a particular bank affiliate or group of bank affiliates are depressed, the remaining affiliate banks may provide offsetting income. If the holding company controls various nonbanking subsidiaries, this counter-cyclical effect could be even more beneficial. These effects could assure greater stability in overall company performance.

Bank management, whose ultimate goal is to maximize the return to its shareholders, realizes there are several potential economic advantages which theoretically could accrue to a holding company bank. For example, certain operational economies of scale might be realized resulting in lower unit costs. Trust services and data processing are good examples where a holding company might realize scale economies. These economies theoretically would not be as readily available to small independent banks. These lower unit costs could contribute to a bank's overall profitability and to the bank's earning potential. In addition, it might be possible to provide specialized skills, such as leasing, which cannot be justified economically for an independent bank.

There are several potential public benefits which might accompany MBHC development. First, MBHCs can benefit a specific market area by offering new or improved financial services. For example, a small independent bank may not be able to offer the breadth and depth of financial services a MBHC can provide. Also, the existence of a greater mobility of funds between holding company affiliates may ensure that necessary funds are available in a specific market area when bank customers demand them. A particular MBHC bank with surplus funds could provide their funds to an affiliate bank in temporary need of funds. Finally, since holding companies have the ability to attract short term funds, it is possible that they could maintain lower liquidity levels and higher loan to deposit ratios within the holding company than a similar number of smaller independent banks could achieve.

The offering of new or improved financial services and the infusion of funds into a particular market area could result in competition which benefits the consumer and business sectors of our society. It is possible that holding companies could offer a more complete array of banking services along with increased credit availability through the more efficient application of scarce funds.

Counterbalancing these potential advantages to MBHCs are some significant potential disadvantages. A common argument is that MBHCs lead to greater concentration of banking resources. This greater concentration could lead to less competition and ultimately to higher prices for banking services. Another possible view is that the existence of absentee owners could be a detriment to the community. The implication here is that a business must be owned by local people in order to serve the community well.

It is also possible that holding companies could drain funds from selected local communities where the return on those funds is not as great as the return in other banking markets. This could severely impact particular rural bank market areas where alternative investment opportunities may not be as lucrative as in more highly industrialized urban market areas.

Carefully designed empirical studies should provide some information which one hopes could enable decision makers to sort out the economic fact from the economic fiction. If performance differences do exist between affiliate and independent banks, it is critical to know what these differences are, what factors account for these differences, and how might these differences ultimately affect the various members of our society. This study is designed to examine these specific issues.

Bank Holding Companies

A bank holding company organization is essentially a form of bank ownership. Any corporation, business trust, association, or similar type of organization which owns or controls one or more banks is classified as a bank holding company. Subsidiary banks (or affiliates) of a bank holding company are independently chartered banks which possess varying degrees of autonomy depending upon the organization and operating policies of the holding company.[2]

One-bank holding companies (i.e., organizations that control only a single bank) must be distinguished from MBHCs which control two or more banks. Both OBHCs and MBHCs are supervised by the Federal Reserve Board. Nevertheless, it is still meaningful to think in terms of MBHCs and OBHCs since some states do not allow holding companies that control more than two banks. MBHCs are establishments that own or control at least 25 percent of the stock of two or more banks. Although MBHCs have existed for approximately three-quarters of a century, they maintained a relatively low profile until the 1960s (Boczar, 1975).

There are two other related forms of multioffice banking organizations. One form is branch banking. The existence or nonexistence of branch banking is determined primarily by state law. A branch bank is a non-main office banking facility that is capable of offering services similar to those of the bank's main office. Given this definition of a branch bank, state laws can be categorized into three broad categories: (1) laws that permit the establishment of branches throughout the state (statewide branch banking); (2) laws that permit branching within a limited geographic area in a given state (limited branch banking); and (3) laws that prohibit the existence of branches within a state (unit banking) (Mote, 1974). A summary of the current state banking laws appears in table 1-1.

Although the terms statewide, limited, and unit banking[3] are commonly accepted ways to classify banking structure, they are often misleading. For example, some states with unit banking laws permit the

Table 1-1.   Summary of State Branching Laws

Statewide (22)	Limited (17)	Unit (12)
Alaska	Alabama	Colorado
Arizona	Arkansas	Illinois
California	Florida	Kansas
Connecticut	Georgia	Minnesota
Delaware	Indiana	Missouri
District of Columbia	Iowa	Montana
Hawaii	Kentucky	Nebraska
Idaho	Louisiana	North Dakota
Maine	Massachusetts	Oklahoma
Maryland	Michigan	Texas
Nevada	Mississippi	West Virginia
New Jersey	New Hampshire	Wyoming
New York	New Mexico	
North Carolina	Ohio*	
Oregon	Pennsylvania	
Rhode Island	Tennessee	
South Carolina	Wisconsin	
South Dakota		
Utah		
Vermont		
Virginia**		
Washington		

*Will become statewide January 1, 1989
**Limited in terms of *de novo* branches; however, branches may be established anywhere in the state through merger.

Source: *Bank Expansion Quarterly.* Golembe Associates, Inc., Vol. XIV, Third Quarter, 1978.

formation of holding companies and allow chain banking to exist while other unit banking states prohibit the formation of holding companies and allow chain banking. The resulting bank structure often results in a quasi-branching system within any given state.

The fact that certain states specifically prohibit branch banking is of utmost importance to this study. The major reason for the growth and development of MBHCs is that the MBHC organizational form permits banks to some extent to circumvent a state's branching restrictions. If all states permitted branch banking, it is highly unlikely that MBHCs would exist in the numbers and in the relative size they do today.

A second form is chain banking. It consists of common ownership of more than one bank by an individual, partnership, family, or any other group of individuals. It is another means by which two or more individually chartered banks can coordinate their operating policies and bring under centralized control more banking resources than could normally be achieved by independently operating banks.

When enacting the Bank Holding Company Act of 1956, Congress intended that holding companies, with few exceptions, be prevented from acquiring nonbanking subsidiaries. However, subsequent amendments to that act have permitted bank holding companies to undertake activities that are closely related to banking or to the managing or control of a commercial bank. Today there are several nonbanking financial activities that may be conducted by a bank holding company either directly or indirectly through a subsidiary. The most significant nonbanking activities that are currently permitted by the Federal Reserve Board are summarized in figure 1-1.

This study restricts itself to MBHCs, and it does not consider any nonbanking affiliates of holding companies. It examines only this particular bank holding company form of organization. It does not deal directly with the existence of or the consequences of either branch banking or chain banking as a form of multioffice banking.

Development of MBHCs Prior to 1956

Bank holding companies have existed since the turn of the century, developing originally in states that limited or prohibited branch banking.

Figure 1-1.   Most Significant Nonbanking Financial Activities Approved
for Bank Holding Companies

1. Making or acquiring, for its own account or for the account of others, loans and other extensions of credit
2. Operating as an industrial bank
3. Servicing loans and other extensions of credit
4. Performing trust activities
5. Acting as an investment or financial advisor
6. Leasing real and personal property
7. Making equity and debt investments in corporations or projects designed primarily to promote community welfare
8. Providing bookkeeping and data processing services
9. Acting as an insurance agent or broker
10. Acting as an underwriter for credit life insurance and credit accident and health insurance directly related to extensions of credit by the bank holding company system
11. Providing courier services
12. Providing management consulting advice to nonaffiliated banks
13. Sale of money orders, checks, and savings bonds

Source: *Regulation Y*, Board of Governors of the Federal Reserve System, 1978.

Frequently, the early bank holding companies were informal organizations and were often referred to as chain or group banks. By 1925, the bank holding company concept was well recognized in the financial community.

The agricultural problems of the 1920s, along with the trend toward urbanization, created some difficulties for many rural banks. As a result, some owners of small banks favored acquisition by a holding company since acquisition provided an opportunity to become part of a stronger banking organization as well as a ready market for the owner's stock. Although data for these early years of bank holding companies are limited, the peak of this movement was apparently reached in the mid-1920s. By 1929 there were approximately 287 holding companies of various types that controlled more than 10 percent of the banking offices in the nation and an estimated 23 percent of the dollar volume of all bank deposits (Ware, 1969).

By year-end 1931, there were 97 bank groups controlling three or more banks. The bank holding company legislation of 1933, coupled with the liberalization of the laws concerning branching activities in several states, resulted in further declines in bank groups. By 1936 there were 52 bank groups (controlling three or more banks) with 14 percent of the deposits of all insured banks, but by 1945 the number of groups fell to 33. In 1954, on the basis of a more inclusive definition (bank groups controlling 25 percent of two or more banks), there were 46 bank holding companies, accounting for only 8 percent of the deposits at all insured banks (Ware, 1969).

Development of MBHCs since 1956

Since 1956 MBHCs have become an increasingly significant element in the American banking system. At year-end 1965 there were 53 bank holding companies in the United States, and they controlled approximately 8 percent of all commercial bank deposits. Since 1965, these companies have grown very rapidly; by 1973 these numbers had increased dramatically to 251 and 35.1 percent respectively (Mayne, 1977).

Much of the MBHC growth since 1965 occurred after 1970, with total offices of MBHCs more than doubling and their total deposits nearly tripling for the 1970–73 period. Table 1-2 and figure 1-2 highlight this growth through 1977. Table 1-2 highlights the growth in the number of MBHCs, the number of banks controlled by MBHCs, and the deposits controlled by these MBHCs for the same period. Figure 1-2 plots the percentage of U.S. offices and deposits held by MBHC banks between 1956 and 1977 and breaks the overall historical development of the holding company movement into various stages.

The growth of MBHCs has been geographically widespread, with MBHCs having increased their share of offices and/or deposits in 32 states in the period 1965–76. As of December 31, 1973, multibank groups controlled over 30 percent of bank deposits in each of 24 states. Today, MBHCs are the most important type of banking organizations in seventeen states and are rapidly increasing in seven other states.[4]

Tables 1-3 and 1-4 identify the states with the most MBHC activity from 1965 to 1973. Table 1-3 highlights in descending order those states where MBHCs have experienced significant gains in deposit shares for the 1965–73 time period. MBHCs in New York head the list with a percentage increase of 70.4 percent. Five other states experienced deposit gains greater than 50 percent while a dozen states had gains in excess of 33 percent. Table 1-4 illustrates which groups of MBHCs by state experienced the greatest growth in the number of offices for the same period.

Table 1-2.   Banking Deposits of Banks in MBHCs for U.S.*

End of Year	Number of Companies**	Number of Banks	U.S. Total Deposits ($ millions)	
			Total	% of U.S.
1956	49	428	14,843	7.5
1960	42	426	18,274	8.0
1965	53	468	27,560	8.3
1966	58	561	41,081	11.6
1967	65	603	49,827	12.6
1968	71	629	57,634	13.2
1969	86	723	62,574	14.3
1970	111	895	78,064	16.2
1971	138	1,106	129,492	24.0
1972	181	1,401	192,448	31.2
1973	251	1,726	233,291	35.1
1974	276	2,122	287,381	38.4
1975	289	2,264	297,472	37.8
1976	298	2,295	286,514	34.2
1977	306	2,301	410,761	36.3

*Partnerships and cases of one bank owning another bank are *not* counted as multibank holding companies for 1971, 1972 and 1973 so that the entire data series is consistent with the pre-1970 Bank Holding Company Act of 1956 Amendment definition of a bank holding company.
**Number of companies represents separate bank groups; that is, tiered holding companies are only counted once.

Source: August editions of the *Federal Reserve Bulletin,* 1967–73; *Annual Statistical Digest,* Board of Governors of the Federal Reserve System, 1967–77.

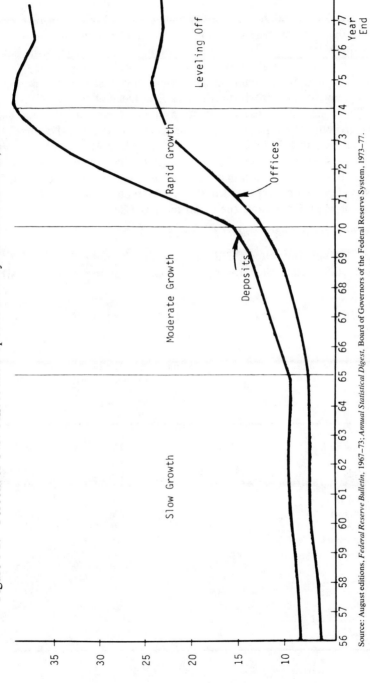

Figure 1-2. Percent of U.S. Offices and Deposits Held by Banks in MBHCs, 1956–77

Slow Growth

Moderate Growth

Rapid Growth

Leveling Off

Offices

Deposits

Year End

Source: August editions, *Federal Reserve Bulletin*, 1967–73; *Annual Statistical Digest*, Board of Governors of the Federal Reserve System, 1973–77.

Maine ranks first with 61.1 percent while New York, Florida, Virginia, and Alabama all recorded gains in excess of 40 percent. On a percentage basis the MBHC gains were more dramatic in deposit growth than they were for increases in the number of state offices. Table 1-5 highlights the number of holding companies, the number of offices, and the percentages of total deposits held by those MBHCs as of December 31, 1977.

These statistics clearly indicate a need to consider the implications of the growth of MBHCs in any evaluation of the structural changes taking place in American banking. The future growth of MBHC expansion may be relatively strong, especially in those states like Texas where multibank activity has not reached a mature state of development. Increased future activity can also be expected if states which currently prohibit the foundation of MBHCs remove their ban on MBHCs.

Reasons for Holding Company Growth

Several reasons are cited for the increase in the number of holding companies. As noted earlier, the primary reason for the growth of MBHCs

Table 1-3.   Most Active Multibank Holding Company States by Deposits

State	Percentage Point Increase in MBHC Share of State Deposits		
	1965–70	1970–73	1965–73
New York	17.7	52.7	70.4
Florida	38.5	24.8	63.3
Maine	41.2	21.0	62.2
Massachusetts	2.1	53.1	55.2
Alabama	0.0	52.1	52.1
Virginia	21.1	30.9	52.0
Missouri	23.7	26.0	49.7
Tennessee	5.7	40.1	45.8
Texas	6.9	30.5	37.4
New Mexico	6.9	30.6	37.5
Colorado	29.2	7.7	36.9
New Jersey	16.8	16.7	33.5
Ohio	11.5	15.1	26.6
Connecticut	3.5	20.7	24.2
Maryland	7.5	16.2	23.7

Source: August editions of the *Federal Reserve Bulletin*, 1965–73.

Table 1-4.   Most Active Multibank Holding Company States by Offices

State	Percentage Point Increase in MBHC Share of State Offices		
	1967–70	1970–73	1965–73
Maine	42.7	18.4	61.1
New York	17.7	39.6	57.3
Florida	25.7	24.0	49.7
Virginia	21.1	25.1	46.2
Alabama	0.0	40.7	40.7
Massachusetts	1.4	27.9	29.3
Tennessee	4.8	23.5	28.3
New Jersey	12.2	15.7	27.9
New Mexico	6.8	20.0	26.8
Ohio	10.6	14.5	25.1
Colorado	13.6	9.0	22.6
Maryland	5.9	16.5	22.4
Missouri	6.4	15.2	21.6

Source: August editions of the *Federal Reserve Bulletin*, 1965–73.

is that they have been an effective way to circumvent the branch banking restrictions that exist in many states. Two additional reasons that are often cited were the desire by banks to expand into approved nonbanking activities and to expand the market area for their banking services. Conversely, the primary reason cited for the growth in OBHCs is that the OBHC corporate structure possesses significant tax advantages for the owners of that corporation.

Additional reasons have been offered for the overall growth and development of bank holding companies. First, it was believed that over the past several decades commercial banks have felt increasing competitive pressures and an increasing customer demand for a wider variety of services. To react to these pressures and to finance these demands during periods of credit restraint (e.g., the late 1960s), they turned to bank holding companies to supplement their funds. An example of this was the use of the holding company to sell commercial paper.

Secondly, in order to provide an increasing variety of services, some banks wanted to enter product and geographic markets from which they were barred by law or regulation. One-bank holding companies provided

Table 1-5.   Banking Offices and Deposits of Banks
in Multibank Holding Company Groups, December 31, 1977

State	Type of Branching	No. of Companies*	No. of Offices**			Total Deposits % of State
			Banks	Branches	Total	
Alabama	L	8	66	336	402	59.6
Arizona	S	1	1	135	136	28.1
Arkansas	L	2	6	26	32	9.4
California	S	8	15	583	598	10.2
Colorado	U	13	102	39	141	65.8
Connecticut	S	5	14	241	255	41.2
District of Columbia	S	1	1	17	18	9.3
Florida	L	29	386	347	733	70.7
Georgia	L	4	26	301	327	45.5
Hawaii	S	1	1	12	13	8.5
Idaho	S	3	4	118	122	48.1
Illinois	U	2	5	0	5	0.1
Indiana	L	1	2	12	14	.01
Iowa	L	11	69	155	224	25.8
Kansas	U	6	11	11	22	4.4
Kentucky	L	1	2	48	50	9.3
Louisiana	L	1	3	3	6	.01
Maine	S	5	24	215	239	68.1
Maryland	S	4	19	268	287	32.9
Massachusetts	L	15	61	670	731	83.2
Michigan	L	23	121	977	1098	67.4
Minnesota	U	8	141	39	180	58.4
Missouri	U	26	220	189	409	61.3
Montana	U	5	41	11	52	54.5
Nebraska	U	1	5	21	26	8.1
Nevada	S	1	2	56	58	50.1

State					
New Hampshire	L	4	16	38	54	32.6
New Jersey	S	8	37	548	585	38.3
New Mexico	L	4	26	98	124	48.6
New York	S	18	74	2160	2234	39.7
North Carolina	S	1	4	71	75	3.3
North Dakota	U	3	32	39	71	35.5
Ohio	L	13	143	995	1138	60.3
Oklahoma	U	3	5	2	7	1.3
Oregon	S	1	1	151	152	35.6
Pennsylvania	L	2	4	2	6	0.1
South Carolina	S	1	1	67	77	43.1
South Dakota	S	3	16	61	77	43.1
Tennessee	L	11	55	336	391	43.8
Texas	U	32	249	72	321	57.6
Utah	S	6	19	179	198	76.3
Virginia	S	13	109	995	1104	75.6
Washington	S	2	3	155	158	14.6
West Virginia	U	1	2	2	4	0.1
Wisconsin	L	22	132	181	313	49.2
Wyoming	U	5	25	0	25	41.0

Totals by State Branching Classification

Branching Category					
Statewide Branching	82	345	6032	6377	38.5
Limited Branching	154	1118	4525	5643	37.9
Unit Banking	105	838	425	1263	29.5

S = statewide branching
L = limited statewide branching
U = unit banking

*Some states like Illinois currently prohibit MBHCs; the companies recorded in this table for those states may have existed prior to this prohibition.
**In many unit banking states some limited service facilities are permitted by law. While these facilities are not branches they appear to have been counted as offices by the regulatory agency.

Source: *Annual Statistical Digest*, Board of Governors of the Federal Reserve System, 1973–77.

a mechanism to expand their services into nonbanking businesses and across state lines.

Legislation Affecting Bank Holding Companies

The Banking Act of 1933 granted the Federal Reserve Board limited powers to regulate bank holding companies controlling the majority of the stock of at least one member bank. Supervisory powers over such an organization's financial policies were intended to protect the bank's depositors, but the Banking Act of 1933 did not set forth guidelines for regulating the formation or expansion of bank holding companies.

The Bank Holding Company Act of 1956 represented the first significant attempt by Congress to subject the formation and expansion of holding companies to federal regulation. The major provisions of the act were designed to define bank holding companies, to prevent any additional geographic expansion, and to require divestment of their nonbanking interests (Fischer, 1961).

The act required a holding company to register with the Federal Reserve Board if it owned 25 percent or more of the stock of each of two or more banks. The act gave the Board the authority to approve or deny applications for the formation of new bank holding companies as well as applications for acquisitions of additional banks by existing bank holding companies. It listed specific factors that the Board was to consider when evaluating a proposed acquisition of a bank. These factors are summarized as follows:

1. The financial history and condition of the bank holding company and the bank concerned
2. The earning prospects of the holding company and the bank concerned
3. The character of bank management
4. The convenience and needs of the communities to be served
5. The preservation of competition in the banking industry[5]

While the primary purposes of the act were to prevent the undue concentration of banks by bank holding companies and to preserve the historical separation between banks and commerce, some feel that the act failed to achieve either purpose. One reason frequently given was the way the act defined a bank holding company.[6] Another reason given was that OBHCs could enter into various nonbanking types of business while MBHCs were restricted in their subsidiary activities.

The Banking Holding Company Act of 1956 was subsequently amended in 1966 and 1970. The 1966 amendments enhanced and expanded the competitive factors that the Federal Reserve Board would use in deciding whether or not to approve a specific request for a bank acquisition. In addition, the 1966 amendment effectively stimulated MBHC activity in two specific ways. It eliminated the 2 percent tax on the filing of a consolidated return, and it made both upstream and downstream loans easier to achieve within the holding company. The 1970 amendments effectively included OBHCs under the act.

In summary, the Bank Holding Company Act of 1956, as amended in 1966 and 1970, attempted to control bank holding company expansion in order to avoid the creation of monopoly or restraint of trade in banking and to allow bank holding companies to expand into nonbanking activities that are related to banking while maintaining a separation between banking and commerce. The latter reflected a long accepted policy of Congress that the "public interest" aspects of banking require a clear separation of banking from other unrelated activity.

To limit interstate banking operations by holding companies, the act provides that a holding company operating in one state may not acquire a bank in a second state unless the second state expressly authorizes such acquisition by statute.

In addition to the federal legislation previously cited, several states have enacted bank holding company legislation. By 1976, 22 states and the District of Columbia placed no limits on the acquisition of bank stock by corporations, while ten states required some form of state approval of bank acquisitions by corporations and twenty states restricted the practice in some way. Table 1-6 identifies which states permit, restrict, and prohibit the formation of MBHCs.

Regulation and Supervision of Bank Holding Companies

Before acquiring more than 5 percent of the shares of any bank, a bank holding company must obtain prior approval of the Federal Reserve Board. The Board may not approve any acquisition that would result in a monopoly or that would substantially lessen competition, unless the anticompetitive effects are clearly outweighed by the acquisition's favorable impact on the banking needs of the community.

In assessing the competitive impact of a proposed acquisition of a bank by a holding company, the Board usually focuses on the relevant local banking markets, for it is in these markets that bank customers may have the fewest alternatives. This determination depends on the total number of banks in the market, but more importantly on the market shares already within the holding company's family of banks as well as on the shares held by the bank to be acquired.

Table 1-6. Classification of State Laws Affecting the Acquisition of Bank Stocks by Corporations*

States which Place No Limitations on MBHC	States which Require State Approval of MBHC Acquisitions	States which Restrict MBHC Acquisition**	States which Prohibit MBHC Formation
Alabama	California	Alaska	Arkansas
Arizona	Connecticut	Georgia	Illinois
Colorado	Florida	Indiana	Kansas
Delaware	Iowa	Iowa	Louisiana
District of Columbia	Maine	Kentucky	Mississippi
Hawaii	Massachusetts	Missouri	Oklahoma
Idaho	Missouri	Nebraska	West Virginia
Maryland	New York	New Hampshire	
Michigan	Oregon	New Jersey	
Minnesota	South Carolina	Pennsylvania	
Montana		Rhode Island	
Nevada		Vermont	
New Mexico		Washington	
North Carolina			
North Dakota			
Ohio			
South Dakota			
Tennessee			
Texas			
Utah			
Virginia			
Wisconsin			
Wyoming			

Note: Iowa and Missouri are listed twice, since their state laws fall into two of the categories.

*As of May 31, 1976.

**The states of Indiana, Kentucky, Nebraska, and Pennsylvania prohibit MBHC acquisitions by law. The remaining states restrict their activity in some way.

Source: Association of Bank Holding Companies, "Bank Holding Company Facts," Spring, 1976 edition.

If the holding company is not already represented in the market of the bank to be acquired, the Board assesses the likely effects of the acquisition on future competition. In making this assessment, the board judges first the possibility that a holding company might enter the market with a *de novo*[7] bank should the proposed acquisition be denied. Second, it determines, on the basis of the present structure of the market, the extent to which *de novo* entry into the market is needed.

In addition to antimonopoly and competitive considerations, the Board also assesses the likely effect of a proposed acquisition on the convenience and banking needs of the public. The Board considers how any proposed bank acquisition is likely to affect the financial and managerial resources of the bank to be acquired and of the holding company. Important factors bearing on its final decision are:

1. The present capital position of the bank and of existing bank subsidiaries, and what plans the holding company has to augment the capital of the bank of its existing subsidiaries, if deficient
2. The quality of the bank's management and any plan the holding company may have for improving it
3. How the holding company intends to finance the acquisition
4. The holding company's debt and its ability to service such debt[8]

Overview and Organization of the Study

The rapid expansion of MBHCs in recent years and the changes in banking structures and practices brought about by this development have generated a significant level of controversy regarding the merits and desirability of holding companies. This controversy has placed a great deal of pressure on the Federal Reserve Board. When determining whether a holding company can acquire control of an individual bank, it must weigh what the ultimate effects will be on competition, public benefits, the convenience and needs of communities for banking and related subsidiaries of bank holding companies, the safety and soundness of banking, and the concentration of banking resources. It is no surprise then that the Federal Reserve Board and the other federal regulatory agencies have maintained a high degree of interest in the relative performance of acquired holding company affiliates over time.

Prior to 1965 the growth of MBHCs paralleled that of the banking system as a whole. However, over the past thirteen years, MBHCs have expanded much more rapidly than the banking system as a whole. The reason for this change is that certain legal, judicial, and regulatory decisions have established new parameters for the development of MBHCs.

Specific economic arguments have been summarized which suggest that this structural change could have some potential benefits as well as some social costs associated with it.

Chapter 2 of this study will review the issues associated with MBHC performance. Several previous MBHC performance studies will be reviewed. Finally, the theoretical foundation for this analysis of MBHC performance will be presented.

Chapter 3 deals with developing the methodology which is to be used to test empirically for performance differences between affiliate and independent banks. Initially, a section will be devoted to identifying how this particular study is a more complete and more rigorous extension of the MBHC performance literature. A specific multivariate methodology will be defined and presented. Various multivariate research techniques will be used to identify what performance differences, if any, exist for a set of test periods. These periods will be long enough to encompass diverse economic conditions and monetary policies.

The results of these empirical tests will be presented in chapter 4. A sample of 155 banks acquired by holding companies from 1968 through 1972 will be examined. A control group of 155 independent banks of similar size in similar geographic locations will be established in an attempt to reduce the influence of extraneous variables to isolate the impact of performance differences. A discussion of the results of these empirical tests conducted for the period 1965–77 will be presented.

Chapter 5 will summarize the major findings of the study and pertinent conclusions drawn from the empirical analysis will be identified. The contributions, implications, and limitations of the study will be discussed. Areas for future research will be highlighted and discussed.

2

Review of Previous Studies on MBHC Performance

The literature relating to the question of bank holding company[1] performance is extensive. Previous empirical studies have investigated many of the various aspects associated with the ultimate effects of bank holding companies on the U.S. banking system. These studies have examined the effects of MBHCs on such diverse issues as banking concentration and competition, the efficiency of trust department operations, and the variability of deposits. However, the specific literature reviewed in this section restricts itself to the changes in bank performance which result from MBHC formations and acquisitions.

Previous studies have developed both the theoretical arguments for and the empirical evidence on what effects bank holding companies have on bank performance. Several of these research efforts have been helpful in forming the foundation for this study. First, the potential impacts of the holding company movement upon bank performance will be summarized. Next, a review of the literature dealing with previously conducted performance studies will be provided. These studies will be discussed in terms of both the univariate and the multivariate research applications which have been used to investigate what effects a bank holding company may have on bank performance. This review is intended to highlight the strengths and the shortcomings of these studies and to identify how this study extends the existing body of knowledge relative to bank holding company performance. Finally, a discussion of the theoretical foundation upon which this bank performance study is based will be presented.

Issues Associated with MBHC Performance

The primary issue associated with this study is whether or not the creation and growth of MBHCs affects the subsequent performance of their affiliate banks. For comparison purposes the performance of affiliate and independent banks operating within the same market area will be examined over various time periods.

The previously developed literature on this subject suggests that both the supporters and the critics of the holding company movement are in general agreement that acquisitions of individual banks by multibank organizations should have significant effects on the financial performance of those banks. Pete Rose and Donald Fraser (1973) argue that it is widely believed that holding companies affect the operating efficiency, capital adequacy, quality of services offered, asset composition, and volume of bank credit made available through affiliates. Robert Lawrence (1967) and Samuel Talley (1971) contend that once a bank has been acquired by a holding company, it should be possible to detect significant performance differences in the areas of asset and loan diversification, liquidity management, capital management, pricing of bank services, expense control, and profitability. The justification for these expectations will be summarized.

Asset and Loan Diversification

Since the holding company ordinarily has affiliates in many different geographical locations and since each location normally serves a distinct economic market area, it appears that holding companies are likely to have more diversified asset and loan portfolios than independent banks. If this greater diversification of assets effectively reduces aggregate risk levels, then affiliated banks could be expected to make more credit available to their local market areas while at the same time assuming more risk.

Liquidity Management

Banks acquired by holding companies could also be expected to decrease their holdings of liquid assets because as a result of their holding company affiliation they have gained access to the overall financial resources of the parent company. This could lead to a greater loan to deposit ratio than would otherwise be possible.

Capital Management

The capital position of affiliate banks could be stronger than independent banks since holding companies will generally be larger, better known, and have better access to the capital markets. No doubt the financial resources of the parent company could assist the affiliated bank very easily in time of a liquidity crisis.

Pricing of Bank Services

If holding companies have more efficient operations and are more vigorous competitors, it seems that the prices charged on loans and other services should be lower; and likewise, in those areas where banks are not paying the maximum rate permitted under Regulation Q, the interest paid on time deposits should be higher. In addition, if holding companies are more efficient, they should be able to operate with lower expenses and be in a position to pass the cost savings on to their customers. On the other hand, if the result of holding company acquisitions increases their market power, these banks may set less favorable prices.

Expense Control

It is not sufficiently clear what effect acquisitions by holding companies might have on bank expenses. If holding companies are able to take advantage of economies of scale, operating expenses of acquired banks would fall. On the other hand, operating expenses of acquired banks could be higher if these banks alter their portfolio of assets by acquiring riskier, less liquid assets. Should these banks have higher loan to deposit ratios, then they might also have larger loan losses and greater administrative costs in acquiring and maintaining loans.

Profitability and Growth

Although costs may rise as a result of acquisition, there are several reasons for believing that the profitability of acquired banks will rise. If acquired banks achieve a higher level of operating efficiency, they should be able to retain some of these savings. The higher loan to deposit ratio should translate into higher revenues even after accounting for higher expenses. Return on capital could be enhanced because of a lower capital position. Adoption of more aggressive market policies should also contribute something toward increased profitability. This stronger capital position and increased earnings level should permit them to grow more rapidly than their independent bank counterparts. Alternatively the affiliate banks may be required to pay certain administrative and operational fees to the holding company, which could increase their actual operating expenses. This could result in the holding company reporting increased profitability and the affiliate bank reporting no significant change in profitability; or, in some cases, even reduced profitability figures.

Bank Holding Company Performance

Within the past ten years at least a dozen attempts have been made to research the impact of bank holding companies on bank performance. The majority of these studies were conducted by researchers within the Federal Reserve System. A few have been conducted by individuals in various academic and corporate organizations. Most of the studies have attempted to compare both the "before" and "after" performance and policies of banks acquired by holding companies with the performance of independent banks of about the same size, serving approximately the same market area. Other studies have simply compared the performance and policies of established holding company banks against established, independently operated institutions. Still others have examined the extent to which differences do exist in the performance of individual holding companies while some have looked at the effects of holding company affiliation on *de novo* banks. In most of these studies the various performance measures used were banking ratios computed from call reports and income and dividend reports filled with the appropriate regulatory agencies.

While most of the performance studies have used essentially the same research methodology, the earlier studies were largely univariate studies. More recently, multivariate methods[2] have been applied to this research area. The reasons for the shift from a univariate to a multivariate methodological approach will be discussed in detail later in this chapter. The initial empirical studies that will be discussed suggest there is some evidence of performance differentials between commercial banks acquired by holding companies and independent banks. A review of these studies is useful in forming a foundation for the proposed research.

Univariate Studies: General Discussion

The two most comprehensive nationwide studies of bank holding company performance were by Robert Lawrence and Samuel Talley of the staff of the Board of Governors of the Federal Reserve System. Lawrence (1967) compared the performance of 43 banks acquired by holding companies between the years 1956 and 1963 with 55 independent banks of similar size and location. His statistical analysis involved the computation of means and their standard errors for 32 performance measures. The results were subsequently tested for statistical significance.

Talley (1971) attemped to update Lawrence's findings by examining 82 banks acquired by holding companies and their paired independent banks between 1966 and 1969. The performance of each acquired bank and its paired bank was compared both before and after acquisition by the acquired bank.

Both studies selected banks from many different states in order to reduce any possible regional bias and included a wide range of bank performance measures including composition of assets, capital adequacy, pricing of bank services, expense control, and profitability. Several other studies have been conducted but these were generally more regional in nature and had similar research designs.

Joe McLeary (1968) of the Federal Reserve Bank of Atlanta examined the statistical comparisons of specific performance variables for 82 holding company banks from three southern states and their paired independent banks for the year 1966. Steven Weiss (1969) of the Federal Reserve Bank of Boston studied the performance of eight banking holding company acquisitions in New England from 1956 to 1967. A study completed in the early 1970s by the Federal Reserve Bank of Cleveland examined the performance of 81 merged banks in the Fourth Federal Reserve District for the period 1960–65.

Robert Ware (1973) of the Federal Reserve Bank of Cleveland studied 43 paired comparisons of commercial banks acquired by holding companies in Ohio from 1965 to 1970. Thomas Snider (1973) of the Federal Reserve Bank of Richmond examined the effect of mergers on the lending behavior of 36 rural banks in Virginia. Stuart Hoffman (1976) of the Federal Reserve Bank of Atlanta performed a case study analysis of two Florida multibank holding companies for the period 1972–74.

Jerome Darnell (1977) of the University of Colorado examined in detail the performance of all banks acquired by MBHCs in Colorado between 1964 and 1972 by comparing the performance characteristics of 41 banks three years before acquisition and three years after acquisition. Hugh Hobson, John Masten, and Jacobus Severiens (1978) investigated the performance differences of 61 matched pairs of banks acquired nationwide during 1969. A summary of the time periods, sample sizes, and analytical techniques used in these studies is provided in table 2-1.

Univariate Studies: Results

The various studies cited provide empirical evidence that in certain cases the claims of both holding company critics and supporters can be sustained. Generally these studies are remarkably consistent in finding that affiliated banks hold smaller ratios of cash assets and of U.S. government

Table 2-1. Summary of Univariate MBHC Performance Studies

Author/Publication Date	Time Period of Acquisitions; Number of Performance Measures Used	Sample Size	Methodology/Post-acquisition Interval
Lawrence (1967)	1954–63 32	43 Acquisitions 55 Independents (nationwide)	Computation of means and standard errors Before and after analysis over varying postacquisition intervals
McLeary (1968)	1966–67 11	Small number of paired comparisons (Florida, Georgia, Tennessee)	Computation of means and ranges t-tests conducted one year before and one year after acquisition
Weiss (1969)	1957–67 32	8 Acquisitions (New England)	Before and after analysis over varying postacquisition periods
Talley (1971)	1966–69 18	82 Paired comparisons (nationwide)	Before and after analysis over varying postacquisition intervals
Smith (1971)	1960–65 25	81 Paired comparisons (Fourth Federal Reserve District)	Before and after analysis: One year before and three years after acquisition Computation of means and standard deviations
Ware (1973)	1965–70 27	44 Paired comparisons (Ohio)	Evaluates changes in performance: one year before and three years after acquisition

Snider (1973)	1962–68	36 Rural banks (Virginia)	Computation of mean changes: from three years before and three years after acquisition
	6		
Hoffman (1976)	1972–74	2 Paired comparisons (Florida)	Case study analysis
	29		
Darnell (1976)	1964–72	41 Acquired banks	Before and after analysis: three years before and three years after acquisition Adjusted for industry trend
	20		
Hobson, Masten, Severiens (1978)	1969	61 Paired comparisons (nationwide)	Computation of comparative ratios for one year before and six years after acquisitions

securities than do comparable independent banks. Specifically they found that subsidiary banks hold significantly larger amounts of state and local government securities than do other banks. In regard to loan policies, holding company banks appear to devote a significantly larger share of their deposits to loans as opposed to investments.

There is little evidence in these studies to conclude that holding companies do improve the capital positions of their acquired banks. No conclusive results are offered by these studies on holding company pricing practices. In general, affiliated banks seem to have higher average ratios of service charges to demand deposits and also higher average loan rates. In contrast, average rates paid on thrift deposits also seem higher. But in each case the differences cited are small and relatively insignificant. On balance, the acquisition of a subsidiary bank by a holding company appears to have little predictable impact on that bank's pricing policies.

Some interesting results emerge from these studies relative to expense control. There is very little evidence that expenses like salaries and wages, interest on deposits, or employee benefits are different at acquired banks from at independent banks. One expense category that is larger at holding company banks is "other expenses." Because of the heterogeneous nature of the bank costs lumped in this category, the studies have been unable to identify the sources of these expense differences, however, there may be additional holding company fees and charges levied on each affiliate bank by the holding company. This would offset any potential gains in operating efficiency which acquisition by a bank holding company might bring.

Profitability of holding company affiliates is generally no better than, and in some select cases worse than, independent banks of the same size. While holding company subsidiaries usually hold higher yielding earning assets, their expenses also rise. On balance, however, there is no significant gain in profitability measured relative to either capital or assets. A summary of the findings of the studies completed through 1973 appear in table 2-2.

Some of the more recent research results are noteworthy. Hoffman's case analysis of two Florida MBHC acquisitions concluded that while in many areas the performance of banks affiliated with holding companies differed significantly from that of the independent banks, their performance did not differ significantly from one another. He concluded that the results of his analysis support the general findings of other holding company performance studies (Hoffman, 1976).

More recently the Hobson, Masten, and Severiens study supported earlier findings that holding company banks had higher loan-to-deposit ratios. It also showed that affiliate banks do not improve their profitability

Table 2-2.   Selected Performance Measures for MBHC vs. Independent
Banks

Performance Measures	Relative to Comparable Independent Banks, the Ratio for Holding Company Banks Is...
Composition of Assets:	
Cash Assets/Assets	Lower
Government Securities/Assets	Lower
Municipal Securities/Assets	Higher
Loans/Assets	Higher
Installment Loans/Assets	Higher
Capital Adequacy:	
Capital/Deposits	N.D.*
Expenses:	
Operating Expenses/Assets	N.D.*
"Other" Expenses/Assets	Higher
Prices of Bank Services:	
Service Charges/IPC Demand Deposits	N.D.*
Interest on Time and Savings Deposits/	
Time and Savings Deposits	N.D.*
Interest on Loans/Loans	N.D.*
Profitability:	
Net Current Income/Assets	N.D.*
Operating Revenue/Assets	Higher

*N.D.=no difference

Source: Rose and Fraser (1973)

after acquisition and that, because of a relatively larger dividend payment, there tends to be an erosion of capital strength. They concluded that it appeared that with good management, independent banks could be profitable and could service as local institutions without holding company affiliation (Hobson et al., 1978).

Darnell concluded that his analysis identified several performance characteristics that were altered significantly after banks were acquired by holding companies. Of twenty balance sheet and operating statement ratios used in the study as performance measures, eleven were found to have changed. He concluded that banks acquired by Colorado bank holding companies in recent years have undergone several significant changes in their operating behavior. Even after adjusting his results for industry trends common to all banks in the state, the evidence suggested that the changes were caused primarily by the holding company affiliations (Darnell, 1977).

Univariate Studies: A Critique

Although the research procedures employed in the univariate studies did vary slightly from study to study, they all used the same basic methodology and, not surprisingly, obtained somewhat consistent results. Most have basically concluded that holding company acquisitions have relatively minor effects on performance. Several aspects of the methodology employed in these studies have been criticized in the financial literature. A detailed review of the criticisms of these methodologies follows.

By and large, the previously reviewed studies have measured and evaluated performance of holding company banks based on a group of selected balance sheet and income statement variables and ratios. They have used before-and-after acquisition comparisons of holding company subsidiaries with a control group of unaffiliated banks, assuming that any change in relative performance would presumably be due to the effects of holding company affiliation.

Rodney Johnson and David Meinster (1973) and Paul Jessup (1974) have contended that, in spite of the impressive consistency, these results could be uniformly misleading. Collectively they questioned three aspects of the basic methodology. These aspects were the sampling and pairing procedures; the use of univariate, rather than multivariate, analysis; and the effects of bank size differentials.

The appropriate sampling procedure. Johnson and Meinster (1973) point out that some of the pairings used in the Lawrence (1967) and Talley (1971) studies consisted of banks of various size differences. Bank size could affect the distribution of assets and, moreover, possible size economies of scale could affect expense, liquidity, and profitability ratios. As a result, the comparability of these pairings is questionable; and, therefore, differences that are attributable to size disparities could obscure the observation of differences resulting from holding company affiliation.

Another sampling problem concerns the postacquisition interval. Specifically, the studies of Lawrence (1967) and Talley (1971) employed some observations that had a postacquisition interval of one year. This transition period is not long enough to provide a serious test of the influence of the holding company upon bank operations nor does it offer sufficient time for the bank's customers to respond to improvements in services offered. Conceivably, little significant difference in the performance of acquired versus paired banks would be detected in one year, but as the interval is increased the acquired bank would feel the full effects of the acquisition and perform substantially differently. In addition, observations of various postacquisition intervals are frequently placed in the wrong sample. To the extent that the interval length affects performance the results of tests from such a sample would not be meaningful.

Appropriate type of analysis. Each univariate analysis previously discussed consists of testing individual measures of performance for statistically significant differences. However, while each of the measures might be individually important and while each makes its own contribution to the set, they are not completely unique or independent. Some of the performance measures might be highly correlated with one another and some measures might act differently in combination from how they would if tested separately.

The fact that some of the measures interact with each other, altering the total effect upon overall performance, cannot be detected or accounted for in univariate analysis. Conversely, by testing for statistical significance using multivariate analysis, it is possible to determine which combination of the original set of variables best distinguished between the two groups of acquired and independent banks.

Effect of bank size. Another reason offered as to why typical before-and-after performance studies of affiliate and independent banks have had consistent results is because MBHCs systematically avoid acquisitions of small banks. Jessup contends that the failure of past comparative studies to detect significant changes in operating performance is not surprising when most of the acquired banks are sufficiently large to approach firm and plant operating efficiency. He suggests that past empirical studies analyzing the performance of banks acquired by MBHCs should be replicated to ascertain whether benefits are more evident among smaller acquired banks than among larger banks (Jessup, 1974).

Multivariate Studies: General Discussion

Two specific multivariate research designs have made significant contributions to the bank holding company literature. Johnson and Meinster (1975) attempted to illustrate how a multivariate analysis of bank holding company performance could be performed. Using Lawrence's 1967 study sample of acquired and independent banks, they used survey questionnaires to duplicate Lawrence's postacquisition data. They obtained data on 36 pairs of acquired and nonacquired banks for 20 different measures of performance. In terms of both number of observations and performance variables to be tested, they used a subset of Lawrence's data. Using a stepwise multiple discriminant model, they found that the acquired banks had discriminant scores toward the upper end of the array of values and the independent banks had scores toward the lower end. An analysis of the scaled vectors associated with the various performance measures indicated that the major difference between acquired and independent banks was their pricing behavior. For affiliate banks interest on loans to loans decreased even though loans to assets increased, while the service charges-to-deposits measure was higher for the acquired banks. This difference was reported to be more important than differences in the asset structure of the two groups of banks. They replicated Lawrence's t-test analysis and found the results to be generally consistent with those reported by Lawrence (1967).

As a result of this disparity, they concluded that on the basis of the results of the univariate analysis performed in their research and in earlier studies, the major differences appeared to be concentrated in the asset structure. Their multivariate results produced not similar, but rather entirely different, results. They concluded that these differences confirm the need for multivariate analysis.

Johnson and Meinster also conducted an interval analysis to examine the extent to which the length of the postacquisition interval affects an acquired bank's performance. Again using a subset of Lawrence's data, their results indicate that acquisition by holding companies had a generally favorable effect on bank performance as measured by the balance sheet composition ratios selected. Moreover, this effect continues for at least four years following the acquisition. They found that the length of the postacquisition interval does have an effect on performance. This finding implies that a significant bias was introduced into the earlier studies by mixing observations having different postacquisition intervals (Johnson and Meinster, 1975).

Lucille Mayne (1977) attempted to bring evidence to bear on the issue of whether or not there were significant differences in the operations of bank holding company affiliates and independent banks during 1969–72. Her study compared selected measures of performance of banking affiliates of multibank holding companies with independent banks competing in the same local markets. Her study was not designed to measure performance changes due to acquisition, but rather she used cross-section analysis for each of the four years studied to detect continuing performance differences between independent banks and those which have been subsidiaries of holding companies long enough to assure their assimilation into the particular MBHC system. Using a sample of 656 banks equally divided between independent banks and holding company subsidiaries, she developed eighteen performance equations representing six bank performance dimensions. These dimensions were asset management, deposit management, capital management, pricing, expense control, and profitability.

Her results found distinguishing characteristics between the two classes of banks in their management of the investment portfolio. There appeared to be a greater willingness to assume more risk in order to achieve a greater return on the part of the holding company affiliates. There were some areas of difference in the loan portfolios, with independent banks holding a significantly smaller percentage of residential mortgage loans and a higher proportion of commercial and industrial loans. Affiliate banks exhibited a tendency to economize on capital relative to independent banks. The affiliates also had consistently higher deposit service charges. There was only marginal evidence of greater operating efficiency on the part of subsidiary institutions. She found that differences in compensation and in loan loss experience were in the affiliates' favor. The affiliate banks exhibited better profit performance.

In short, she presented significant evidence of the ability of holding companies to marshal expert management and technological resources with the effects being transmitted through to an affiliate's earnings statements during a period that was generally favorable to aggressive management. These results were more consistent with Johnson and Meinster's results (1975) than with any of the univariate studies conducted (Mayne, 1977).

Other multivariate models have been used to examine related issues in commercial bank performance. In a related performance study, Arthur Fraas of the staff of the Board of Governors uses multiple regression to examine the extent to which differences do exist in the performance of individual holding companies. He found that there was significant differences in the performance of individual holding companies. His results suggested that behavioral differences and alternate management styles were responsible for differences in holding company performance. For many of the performance measures, banks affiliated with particular holding companies are operating in a way which differs significantly from the operations of independent banks but even more from the operations of banks affiliated with other holding companies (Fraas, 1974).

William Jackson of the Federal Reserve Bank of Richmond used a multivariate model to investigate the specific sources of overall commercial bank performance. Using factor analysis, he attempted to isolate the common causality present in what is generally considered to be highly correlated banking data.[3] He identifies thirteen independent dimensions of bank performance, one of which was clearly a bank holding company dimension. His results indicate that holding company affiliation is a key determinant in determining a bank's overall financial performance (Jackson, 1975).

Multivariate Studies: Results

The results of the multivariate tests reviewed yield relatively consistent results. It appears that multibank holding companies have some effect on the asset structure of acquired banks. In addition to holding what is generally regarded to be riskier asset portfolios, the evidence indicates that in some cases MBHC banks exhibit lower capital to asset ratios than comparable independent banks. MBHC banks exhibit significantly higher earnings and expenses subsequent to affiliation while their profitability remains relatively unchanged. In short, MBHC banks acquire riskier portfolios and more leveraged capital positions than do similar independent banks, but their profitability or growth is no different.

However, the multivariate studies do not consistently support and in several cases contradict the univariate studies. Specifically, the Johnson and Meinster study (1975) indicated that one factor which discriminates between affiliate and independent banks is their pricing behavior. The Mayne (1977) study suggested that regardless of which profitability measure is used, affiliate banks are generally more profitable than independent banks. Also, the results of these analyses indicate that a critical factor in interpreting the research results is the length of the postacquisition period used. While univariate studies each used different interval periods for evaluation purposes, Darnell's (1977) three-year period and Hobson et al.'s (1978) seven-year period were the longest. Their results do conflict with the consensus results of the univariate studies that used a shorter period. It appears that different postacquisition intervals can introduce a significant bias in the results and may have obscured to some extent the results of earlier empirical studies.

The limited attempts at using multivariate research techniques do not support or confirm the results of earlier studies. In fact, the findings of the multivariate studies discussed are unique to themselves. No doubt this may be due to important differences in sample size and selection technique, duration of and particular time span studied, and the use of a statistical methodology which permits the researcher to study situations where combinations of variables are involved either as predictors or as measures of performance.

It is widely recognized in the financial management of any institution that the commonly used measures of performance interact with each other, altering their total effect on overall performance. It appears that the use of multivariate analysis is best suited to determine which combination of performance variables best distinguishes between acquired and independent banks. This type of research methodology can measure the relative contribution made by each individual performance measure toward distinguishing between the two predefined groups since some performance measures might perform differently in combination with others than they would if tested separately.

The evidence previously discussed suggests that the multivariate results indicate that the effects of bank holding company affiliation on the performance of an acquired bank may not be as slight as previous univariate studies have concluded. The sampling designs and the practice of combining observations having varying postacquisition interval lengths used in earlier univariate studies may have biased earlier empirical results. The multivariate results indicate that additional research is necessary to overcome these sampling and statistical biases and inconsistencies. A definite need exists for more rigorous and sophisticated research into the area of bank holding company performance.

Theoretical Foundation for the Analysis of Bank Performance

Commercial banks are financial institutions and as such supply financial services to the economic community. Their assets are almost exclusively financial in nature. The composition of their assets distinguishes them from other productive units of the economy whose assets are of a more tangible variety (e.g., plant, equipment, and inventory assets). Banks issue contractual obligations in order to obtain the majority of the funds necessary to purchase their financial assets. In the context of their overall operation, their net worth or reserve position, which results from the sale of stock or the accumulation of earnings, represents a relatively minor source of funds.

Some of the objectives of any financial institution include maximizing the wealth of their shareholders while attempting to fill the diverse needs of both ultimate lenders and ultimate borrowers. In order to provide a theoretical framework which measures how well any financial institution achieves these multiple objectives, basic financial management theories and principles must be applied to the institution being examined.

Financial management can be viewed as a form of applied economics that draws heavily on theoretical economic constructs. It also draws certain principles from accounting, another area of applied economics. The importance of economics to the development of financial management theories can best be described in light of the areas of macroeconomics and microeconomics. Macroeconomics is concerned with the overall institutional environment in which the firm must operate, while microeconomics concerns itself with the determination of optimal operating strategies for the firm.

Since any business concern must operate in the macroeconomic environment, the financial manager must be aware of the consequences of varying levels of economic activity and changes in economic policy. The theory of microeconomics provides for the efficient operation of a firm. The principles involved in supply and demand relationships, economies of scale differentials, cost and revenue curve analysis, and various profit maximizing strategies are drawn from microeconomic theory. In this light, financial management has emerged as a separate branch of economics.

Since the scope of financial management can be defined to cover decisions about both the use and the acquisition of funds, a principal content of that subject is concerned with how well financial management makes judgments about the acquisition and application of funds. In short, how can financial performance be measured and evaluated?

The analysis of financial performance has typically been devoted to the calculation of ratios in order to evaluate the past, current, and projected performance of the firm. These ratios provide relative measures of the firm's performance. The basic inputs for this type of financial analysis are the firm's income statement and balance sheet.

The theoretical support for this study draws heavily from basic macroeconomic and microeconomic theory. It attempts to apply fundamental financial management principles to the measurement of the relative performance differences of two groups of commercial banks. It uses reported financial information to determine if one particular type of a commercial bank, an MBHC affiliate bank, performs any differently from an independent bank competitor once it has been acquired by a specific bank holding company. Any relative performance differences are examined to determine what fundamental economic and financial principles justify these differences. Finally, the public policy consequences are examined in order to determine what future banking structure changes would be most desirable for our society.

3

Research Design

This chapter is devoted to establishing a basic research design and methodology which is offered as a logical extension of earlier bank holding company performance studies. Multivariate research techniques will be applied to a nationwide sample of 310 commercial banks. One hundred and fifty-five carefully selected matched pairs of MBHC affiliate and independent banks[1] have been selected for comparison and control purposes. These banks have been grouped into the five relatively homogeneous size categories identified in table 3-1 for comparison purposes. Data have been collected for a 14-year period, 1964–77. The study is designed to permit performance comparisons to be made over postacquisition intervals ranging from five to nine years in length. Some 76 performance measures have been defined and will be utilized initially for comparison purposes.

Chapter 2 reviewed earlier performance studies and summarized how they attempted to measure and evaluate the performance of holding company banks. It was noted that many of these studies were similar in their research design. They have employed one of two basic investigative procedures: a before-and-after performance analysis or a cross-section time series analysis of performance. Both procedures generally used a paired sampling technique with independent banks.

Table 3-1. Bank Size Categories

Category	Asset Size ($M)
1	0–10
2	11–25
3	26–50
4	51–100
5	101–500

This study does not employ the same type of before-and-after approach as earlier studies. The use of relatively short preacquisition and postacquisition intervals was avoided. It is not desirable to have test intervals so short that it becomes difficult to determine whether or not any observed performance differences were subsequently maintained or eroded by various competitive pressures. The study employs principal components analysis and multiple discriminant analysis to determine what, if any, performance differences do exist over time once a bank has been acquired by a MBHC.

The study will also examine the issue of whether or not any performance differences are a continuation of an established performance trend gained prior to acquisition. Should performance differences appear after acquisition, but not before, then it is highly probable that the changes are, in part, due to the bank's acquisition by a holding company.

This research is offered as a more complete and more rigorous extension of earlier MBHC performance studies. Specifically, this research design

1. Contains a sample of banks that is national in scope and is larger than any previous study undertaken to test for performance differences;
2. Examines MBHC acquisitions for a five-year period, 1968–72, during which there had been both moderate and rapid growth associated with the MBHC movement;
3. Segments the acquired banks into five distinct size categories and examines each size category for possible performance differences;
4. Employs multivariate descriptive and inferential techniques to investigate the use of various combinations of performance variables to be used as predictors or as measures of performance;
5. Uses financial data collected for a 14-year period which permits performance comparisons over lengthy postacquisition intervals and other diverse economic conditions and monetary policies; and
6. Contains pairs of banks which have been very carefully related as to size, location, and basic sources and uses of funds.

Data Base

This study uses multivariate techniques to investigate the performance differences between MBHC affiliate and independent banks. Since changes in any select group of banks might reflect changes over time for all commercial banks, two groups of banks will be used. Specifically, each of 155 acquired bank selections were made on the basis of aggregate bank size, bank market area, general balance sheet characteristics, and, whenever possible, status of Federal Reserve membership.

Matched pairs were determined by examining defined bank market areas[2] for each acquired bank. All paired banks are from the same market areas. An attempt was made to select an independent bank of similar size, with similar balance sheet ratios,[3] and whenever possible with similar membership status in the Federal Reserve System.[4] Tables 3-2 and 3-3 present the frequency distribution and other descriptive statistics relating to total asset size for both bank groups. Table 3-2 illustrates that all but 14 of the matched pairs had total assets less than $50 million and only one matched pair had total assets in excess of $100 million. Over half of the matched pairs (56.8 percent) had total assets between $11 million and $50 million. Table 3-3 indicates that the measures of central tendency and the levels of dispersion for the affiliate and independent banks within each size category are roughly equal.

A list of approved bank holding company acquisitions for the period 1968 to 1972 was obtained from the Federal Reserve Board. Subsequently, any OBHC related acquisitions were excluded from the list. In addition, all *de novo* acquisitions were removed from the list.[5] One bank holding company's acquisitions were excluded because affiliate banks that were previously part of an OBHC could exhibit significant performance differences from other acquired banks and because the study is limited to MBHC performance. *De novo* acquisitions were not included because newly chartered banks would have no prior performance profile and could not be investigated for subsequent performance changes.

One remaining type of acquisition was removed from the sample of

Table 3-2.   Frequency Distribution

Total Assets ($M)	Absolute Frequency		Relative Frequency (%)	
	Affiliate Banks	Independent Banks	Affiliate Banks	Independent Banks
0–10	53	53	34.2	34.2
11–25	62	62	40.0	40.0
26–50	26	26	16.8	16.8
50–100	13	13	8.4	8.4
101–500	1	1	.6	.6
Total	155	155	100.0	100.0

Table 3-3.   Descriptive Statistics

Total Assets ($M)	Affiliate Banks	Independent Banks
$0–10 M		
Mean	$ 6.87 M	$ 6.49 M
Standard Deviation	2.751	2.617
Range	$ 1.7–10.8 M	$ 1.7–10.9 M
$11–25 M		
Mean	$17.68 M	$17.69 M
Standard Deviation	4.049	4.619
Range	$11–23.7 M	$11.1–25 M
$26–50 M		
Mean	$37.65 M	$36.98 M
Standard Deviation	8.082	8.183
Range	$26.6–48.6 M	$26.8–48.6 M
$51–100 M		
Mean	$76.81 M	$73.76 M
Standard Deviation	12.929	10.689
Range	$56.4–94.4 M	$55–95.7 M
$100–500 M		
Mean	$157.1 M	$177 M
Standard Deviation	...	...
Range	...	...

acquisitions. Any apparent "lead banks" of a bank holding company were excluded. In each holding company traditionally there is a "lead bank" which is usually the largest, most dominant bank in the holding company. It is unlikely that these banks would subsequently see their performance change as a result of their holding company affiliation. In fact, often times it could be the "lead bank's" performance qualities that are passed on to the smaller, less dominant banks in the holding company. To remove any "lead banks" involved in acquisitions, the following decision rule was employed:

Purge the largest acquired bank from each individual holding company that has:

1. The earliest date of acquisition, and
2. Is greater than $100M, or
3. Is five times larger than its first acquisition.

After this screening procedure was completed, 733 affiliate banks were identified. A summary of this screening procedure appears in figure 3-1.

Using the procedure described earlier, an attempt was made to find a paired independent bank for each of these banks. To be included as a paired independent bank, a bank had to remain in existence during the entire test period and was not subsequently acquired by another holding company. One hundred and fifty-five pairs of banks were ultimately included in this newly defined universe.

The time period 1968–72 was selected for two reasons. First, the five-year period covers diverse economic conditions and varying levels of acquisition activity. Second, the period allows for postacquisition intervals of from nine years for banks acquired in 1968 to five years for banks acquired in 1972. It was assumed that any performance differences that would appear after acquisition would have appeared or would begin to appear during this time interval. Financial data for these banks were obtained from the year-end of Reports of Condition and Reports of Income and Dividends obtained from the Federal Reserve Deposit Insurance Corporation and the Federal Reserve System.

Table 3-4 identifies the final composition of the MBHC acquisitions while table 3-5 highlights the composition by state and year of acquisition. The MBHC acquisitions in 1970 and 1971 constitute approximately 58 percent of the total acquisitions identified in this study. Those MBHC acquisitions made in 1968 were only approximately six percent of the total. Although the banks were drawn from 25 different states, the states of Colorado, Florida, Missouri, Ohio, Texas, and Wisconsin provided approximately 75 percent of the total. Texas was the state most often represented in the study.

Figure 3-1. Test Sample Screening Results

	Number of Banks
Total Number of Bank Holding Company Acquisitions Approved	1845*
De Novo Acquisitions Made by MBHCs	– 82
One-Bank Holding Company Acquisitions	–937
"Lead Banks" Counted in Approved Acquisitions	– 93
	733

*All data are for 1968-72

Table 3-4. MBHC Acquisitions by Size and Year of Acquisition

Size	1968	1969	1970	1971	1972	Total
<10M	8	12	17	13	3	53
11–25M	1	10	17	19	16	62
26–50M	1	1	9	8	7	26
51–100M	0	2	3	4	4	13
100–500M	0	0	1	0	0	1
Total	10	25	46	44	30	155

Research Objectives and Statement of Hypotheses

The research objectives of the study are presented below. The purpose is to determine whether or not holding company affiliate banks perform any differently, once they have been acquired, from comparable independent banks. Should specific performance differences exist, an attempt will be made to identify the factors which account for these differences and to determine what public policy implications might exist relative to banking structure in the United States.

The primary research objectives are presented in figure 3-2 and, where appropriate, the specific statistical hypotheses are stated in the null form.

Performance Measures Defined

Bank management and financial management theory has identified many financial ratios which can be used to identify the past, current, and projected performance of a financial institution. Ratio analysis provides the most common form of financial analysis used for this purpose. It identifies alternate measures of the firm's performance that can be used for comparison purposes. The basic inputs to this type of financial analysis are the firm's balance sheet and income statements.

In the financial analysis of a commercial bank, many financial ratios have been offered as measures of different aspects of bank performance. Previous performance studies traditionally aggregated these ratios into the performance dimensions of asset composition, liquidity, deposit mix, capital management, profitability, and growth. After identifying the availability of the financial data that was common to all year-end Reports of Condition and Reports of Income and Dividends for the period 1964–77,

Table 3-5.   MBHC Acquisitions by State and Year of Acquisition

State	1968	1969	1970	1971	1972	Total
Alabama	0	0	0	0	2	2
Arkansas	0	0	0	1	0	1
California	0	1	0	0	0	1
Colorado	3	1	2	2	5	13
Connecticut	0	0	1	0	0	1
Florida	0	2	2	17	3	24
Georgia	0	0	1	0	0	1
Iowa	1	0	2	0	4	7
Maine	0	0	1	1	0	2
Maryland	0	0	1	0	0	1
Michigan	0	0	0	0	2	2
Minnesota	1	1	1	1	1	5
Missouri	0	3	6	8	3	20
Montana	0	1	0	0	0	1
New Jersey	0	0	1	0	0	1
New Mexico	0	0	0	2	0	2
New York	0	1	1	0	1	3
North Dakota	1	0	0	0	0	1
Ohio	0	2	8	3	3	16
South Dakota	0	1	0	0	0	1
Tennessee	0	0	1	0	1	2
Texas	2	8	11	2	4	27
Virginia	0	0	3	3	0	6
Wisconsin	2	4	3	4	1	14
Wyoming	0	0	1	0	0	1
Total	10	25	46	44	30	155

76 performance measures were collected for the study.[6] These financial ratios and growth percentages have scaling properties that are appropriate for use in principal components analysis and multiple discriminant analysis. The initial set of performance measures utilized in this study appear in table 3-6.

Research Design

Overview

An attempt has been made in this chapter to identify how this study is a logical extension of earlier MBHC performance studies. The data base

Figure 3-2.   Research Objectives and Hypotheses

Objective 1: To determine if MBHC affiliation has a significant impact on the performance of a commercial bank

> **Hypothesis 1:** The performance of commercial banks is not significantly associated with acquisition by a MBHC.

Objective 2: To determine which available performance measures best discriminate between MBHC affiliate bank performance and independent bank performance

> **Hypothesis 2:** The centroids of the two groups of performance variables are equal.

Objective 3: To determine over what time period any observed performance differences occur

Objective 4: To identify what factors can be attributed to any observed performance difference and to discuss the public policy implications for banking structure

and the performance measures have been defined, and the research objectives and hypotheses have been highlighted. The remaining portion of this chapter will set forth the study's basic research design.

Initially, the significance and importance of employing various data reduction techniques in this research design will be discussed. The basic multivariate assumptions of the study will be identified. Then two multivariate models will be defined and presented. These models are designed to investigate and examine the research objectives and hypotheses.

Importance of Data Reduction

In establishing the use of financial ratios and growth percentages as relative performance measures, it is straightforward to identify one ratio as a measure of liquidity, another as a measure of profitability, and still another as a measure of expense control. However, significance testing is complicated by two related problems: (1) some of the performance measures might be highly correlated with one another, and (2) some measures might act differently in combination from how they would if tested separately (Kerlinger, 1973).

The fact that some of the measures interact upon each other, altering the total effect upon overall performance, cannot be detected or accounted for in any univariate analysis. It is paramount to determine which combination of performance variables best distinguishes between two categorical variables, acquired and independent banks.

There are many instances in the finance literature where data reduction techniques have been utilized prior to conducting various multivariate analyses. Robert Saunders (1969) utilized principal components analysis

Table 3-6.   Performance Measures Used in a Multivariate Analysis of
MBHC Performance

Asset Composition

1.   Liquid Assets*/Total Assets
2.   Risk Assets**/Total Assets
3.   Total Loans/Total Assets
4.   Cash and Due/Total Assets
5.   U.S. Government Securities/Total Assets
6.   Securities of State and Political Subdivisions/Total Assets
7.   Securities of U.S. Government Agencies/Total Assets
8.   U.S. Government Securities + U.S. Government Agency Securities/Total Assets
9.   Other Securities/Total Assets
10.   Earning Assets***/Total Assets
11.   Total Loans/Total Deposits
12.   Consumer Loans/Total Assets
13.   Real Estate Loans/Total Assets
14.   Commercial and Industrial Loans/Total Assets
15.   Farm Loans/Total Assets
16.   Automobile Loans/Total Assets
17.   Real Estate Loans/Total Loans
18.   Commercial and Industrial Loans/Total Loans
19.   Agricultural Loans/Total Loans
20.   Consumer Loans/Total Loans
21.   Automobile Loans/Total Loans
22.   Earning Assets***/Total Deposits

Liquidity

23.   Cash and Due/Demand Deposits, IPC
24.   Cash and Due/Total Deposits
25.   Cash and Due+U.S. Government Securities/Demand Deposits, IPC
26.   Cash and Due+U.S. Government Securities/Total Deposits
27.   Liquid Assets*/Total Deposits
28.   Liquid Assets*/Total Demand Deposits

Deposit Mix

29.   Total Time and Savings Deposits, IPC/Total Deposits
30.   U.S. Government Deposits/Total Deposits
31.   Deposits of State and Political Subdivisions/Total Deposits
32.   Total Demand Deposits/Total Deposits
33.   Total Time Deposits/Total Deposits

Capital Management

34.   Equity Capital/Total Assets
35.   Equity Capital/Risk Assets**
36.   Equity Capital/Total Deposits
37.   Equity Capital/Total Loans
38.   Total Capital Accounts/Total Assets

Table 3-6 *(Continued)*

39. Total Capital Accounts/Risk Assets**
40. Total Capital Accounts/Total Deposits
41. Total Capital Accounts/Total Loans
42. Surplus/Total Deposits
43. Capital + Surplus/Total Deposits

Investing Policy

44. U.S. Government Securities + U.S. Government Agency Securities + State and Political Subdivision Securities/Total Deposits
45. Earning Assets***/Available Funds****
46. U.S. Government Securities/Total Deposits
47. State and Political Subdivision Securities/Total Deposits
48. U.S. Government Securities + U.S. Government Agency Securities/Total Deposits
49. Interest Received on Investments/Total Operating Income

Pricing of Bank Services

50. Service Charges on Deposits/Demand Deposits, IPC
51. Interest and Fee on Loans/Total Loans
52. Interest on U.S. Government Securities/U.S. Government Securities
53. Total Service Charges and Fees/Total Operating Income
54. Service Charges on Deposits/Total Deposits
55. (Interest and Fee on Loans/Total Loans) − (Interest on Deposits/Total Time and Savings Deposits)
56. Interest on Deposits/Total Time and Savings Deposits

Expense Control

57. Total Operating Expense/Total Assets
58. Total Operating Income/Total Assets
59. Total Operating Expense/Total Operating Income
60. Other Operating Expense/Total Assets
61. Other Operating Expense/Total Operating Expense
62. Loan Losses/Total Loans
63. Total Salaries + Employee Benefits/Total Assets
64. Interest Paid on Deposits/Total Assets

Profitability

65. Net Income/Total Assets
66. Net Income/Total Equity Capital
67. Net Operating Income/Total Assets
68. Net Operating Income/Total Equity Capital
69. Net Income/Total Operating Income

Growth

70. Growth in Total Assets
71. Growth in Total Deposits
72. Growth in Total Demand Deposits

Table 3-6 *(Continued)*

73. Growth in Total Time Deposits
74. Growth in Total Savings Deposits
75. Growth in Total Loans
76. Growth in Total Capital Accounts

*Liquid Assets=Cash and Due+U.S. Government Securities+U.S. Agency Securities+Federal Funds Sold
**Risk Assets=Obligations of State and Political Subdivisions+Other Securities Held+Total Loans+Other Assets
***Earning Assets=All Securities Held+Total Loans
****Available Funds=Total Deposits+Federal Funds Purchased

to interpret cross-sectional differences among commercial banks. George Pinches and Kent Mingo (1973) used factor analysis to screen financial data for use in a multiple discriminant analysis of industrial bond ratings. Robert Klemkosky and J. William Petty (1973) used stepwise discriminant analysis to identify those variables with the best discriminating power in an analysis of stock price variability.

Given the performance variables identified earlier in this chapter, the first step in this multivariate research design is to identify a meaningful set of independent variables. Throughout the study, several techniques are used to reduce the dimensionality of the defined set of performance variables. In Model 1, principal components analysis is used to reduce the dimensionality of the performance measures with as little loss of information as possible with the new variables (components) being simply linear combinations of the original ones. In Model 1, an iterative selection procedure is used to find the set of variables that best discriminates between the two groups of acquired and independent banks. Later, stepwise discriminant analysis is used to identify which specific performance variables account for any differences between the two groups of banks in a specific test period.

Multivariate Assumptions and Data Requirements

This study's research design employs three distinct multivariate techniques. Model 1 utilizes principal components analysis (PCA) and multiple discriminant analysis (MDA) to investigate the existence of possible performance differences between affiliate and independent banks. MDA is also used to examine over what time periods these differences appear. Model 2 uses stepwise discrimnant analysis (SDA) to identify specific performance differences that exist for the banks included in this study. SDA is run on all 310 banks in the aggregate and then on each of the five sets[7] of acquired banks and their paired independent banks.

Most multivariate analysis techniques generally can be categorized as either an analysis of interdependence or an analysis of dependence.

PCA is an analysis of interdependence since the objective of the procedure is to give meaning to a given set of variables. Other prominent analyses of interdependence are cluster analysis and multidimensional scaling.

MDA and SDA are analyses of dependence. They involve a variable or set of variables which is explained or predicted by another set of variables. Other common analyses of dependence are multiple regression and canonical correlation.

The use of various multivariate models require that the data have certain scaling properties.[8] PCA involves no explicit independent or dependent variables. It simply evaluates a set of variables that must have interval scaling properties. MDA and SDA involve a dependent variable that must be nominally scaled and independent variables that are metrically scaled. Since all performance variables are either ratios or growth percentages, all multivariate data requirements have been satisfied in this study.

In using MDA and SDA, Pinches and Mingo point out that there are three basic assumptions that must be made for any MDA or SDA analysis. They indicate that (1) the groups must be discrete and known, (2) each observation in each group must be described by a set of measurements of n characteristics or variables, and (3) the n variables must arise from multivariate normal populations (Pinches and Mingo, 1973). For the purposes of this research design, the first two assumptions are clearly met, since the two groups are defined as affiliate and independent banks and since financial ratios have been computed for each bank for each year of the study. Although it is extremely difficult in any research design to prove that the third data requirement has been met, a recent study conducted by Donald Ricketts and Roger Stover supports the use of commercial bank financial ratios in multivariate studies. Their empirical results indicated that, in general, a normality assumption could not be rejected for most commercial bank financial ratios they tested and that these financial ratios were appropriate for most typical univariate and multivariate statistical comparisons (Ricketts and Stover, 1978).

Model 1

Analysis of performance measures. The previously defined hypotheses deal primarily with the possible effects of MBHC affiliation on bank performance. It is important, therefore, that any performance differences between affiliate and independent banks be identified. In addition, if performance differences do exist, it is useful to know over what time periods they appear. In order to test for the existence and statistical significance of any performance differences, multiple discriminant analysis (MDA) was used.

MDA effectively constructs a discriminant function that classifies observations into one of two or more groups based on some set of independent variables. It is typically used in the financial area when group identification is specified in qualitative form (Kerlinger, 1973). In this study the defined groups are acquired and independent banks. In essence, the discriminant function is a regression equation with a dependent variable that represents group membership, or in this case, holding company status.

Prior to describing the application of MDA, it is necessary to discuss the various types of variables used in this study. Both categorical and continuous variables were used. Kerlinger (1973, p. 102) noted the basic differences between the two when he stated that: "A categorical variable is one in which subjects differ in type or in kind. Each subject is assigned to one of a set of mutually exclusive categories that are not ranked. . . . In contrast, a continuous variable is one in which subjects differ in amount or degree. A continuous variable can take on numerical values that form an ordinal, nominal, interval, or ratio scale. In short, a continuous variable expresses gradations, whereas a categorical variable does not."

Two variables in this study are categorical. The first, holding company status, is accounted for by the sets of MBHC acquired banks and their paired independent banks. The second categorical variable is time. It is expressed in a three-year preacquisition interval and by postacquisition intervals which range from five to nine years.

Continuous variables are also considered in the study. These are the 76 performance variables that were defined earlier in this chapter.

Step 1 of the research design. Prior to performing MDA on the various sets of banks being examined in this study an attempt was made to reduce the dimensionality of the performance measures previously defined. Principal components analysis (PCA), a form of factor analysis, was used to reduce the performance data to a new set of variables with as little loss of information as possible. The new variables, or components, that were developed are linear combinations of the original ones. R. J. Rummel specifically points out that PCA is well designed to achieve many research objectives. Some of those cited are to:

1. Untangle complex patterns of intervariable association in data;
2. Reduce the dimensionality of a set of data;
3. Develop a data based unidimensional index that maximally separates groups; and

4. Transform a matrix of predictor variables prior to applying some other technique such as multiple discriminant analysis.[9]

Before describing more specifically the application of PCA in this study, it is necessary to identify the sequence of steps a PCA performs. The PCA method is mathematically satisfying because it yields a mathematically unique solution in any data reduction problem. It extracts a maximum amount of variance as each principal component is calculated. The first principal component extracts the most variance, the second, the next most variance, and so on. The net effect is to reduce the overall dimensionality of the raw data to a finite number of principal components such that each derived principal component is an actual linear composite of the original data and each principal component is uncorrelated with each other (Kerlinger, 1973).

Initially PCA was applied to all 310 banks using year-end 1977 financial data for all 76 performance variables. Statistical Analysis System (SAS) computer programs were used to conduct the PCA. The most recent financial data were used because all acquired banks would have been members of their holding companies for at least five years, and the use of these data should capture any financial differences that existed between their performance and the performance of independent banks by that time.

Step 2. Once the data had been factor analyzed, the primary consideration became the selection of those components to be retained for subsequent multivariate tests. Paul Green suggests a number of procedures for determining how many principal components to retain. According to Green:

1. Run significant tests on the separate eigenvalues in the correlation matrix;
2. Retain all eigenvalues that are greater than unity;
3. Prepare a plot of residuals from the r-th (r is less than n) rank approximation matrix to see if these residuals are small and approximately normally distributed;
4. Prepare a plot of variance accounted for versus the rank number of the extracted components and look for an "elbow" in the graph; and
5. Split the sample in half and retain only those components with high correspondence of factor loadings across the two subsamples.[10]

While these various significance tests can be conducted, the primary interest in this study was the operational significance and the interpretability of the principal components retained. In this light, the decision on what number of principal components to retain was determined jointly by the amount of variance explained by each additional principal component and the overall interpretability of that principal component.

In performing the PCA, the SAS output produced:

1. The simple statistics (means and standard deviations) of the performance variables to be analyzed
2. The correlation matrix of all performance variables
3. The prior estimates of communalities for all performance variables
4. The eigenvalues of the correlation matrix, adjusted for prior estimates of communalities
5. The portion of the total variance explained by each component and the cumulative portion of the total variance explained by all components
6. Eigenvectors
7. Initial factor loadings
8. Plots of all factor patterns
9. The scoring coefficient matrix

Step 3. Once the new principal components were identified, these data were used as inputs into the SAS multiple discriminant analysis procedure to build a discriminant function. As a result of performing MDA on all banks, the SAS output produced:

1. The simple descriptive statistics (mean, sum, variance, frequency and standard deviation) of each performance variable
2. The pooled covariance matrix for each group
3. The within-group correlation matrix for each group
4. The partial correlation coefficients computed from the pooled covariance matrix
5. The discriminant function
6. The classification results for each observation

As a result of these procedures, a single discriminant function was defined. The overall classification results of the discriminant function were evaluated to determine if the observed results were significantly different from a chance classification.

A total efficiency measure of the classification ability of each discriminant function was employed. Maurice Joy and John Tollefson suggest that a total efficiency measure is much preferred to any conditional efficiency measure as an appropriate measure of classification performance (Joy and Tollefson, 1975).

Given a discriminant function, MDA can determine if any differences do exist between the affiliate and independent banks. In order to determine over what time period these differences appeared, the discriminant function was used to classify other data observations associated with the 310 banks.

This use of discriminant analysis as a classification technique can be conducted after all data reduction schemes have been completed and the MDA function has been defined. Once a set of performance variables is found which produces the most satisfactory discriminant function for classifying the affiliate and independent banks, the discriminant coefficients are applied to corresponding measures of performance using year-end data from 1964–76. A combined variable, Z, is obtained for each period. If a test for differences in the two groups based on performance profiles consisting of three different performance measures is performed, the general form of the discriminant function becomes:

$$Z_i = A_1 x_{i,1} + A_2 x_{i,2} + A_3 x_{i,3} = \sum_{j=i} A_j x_{i,j}$$

The $x_{i,j}$s represent the various measures of performance for each observation i, and the A_js represent the discriminant coefficients, or weights, assigned to these measures. An array of Z scores will be obtained when the coefficients are multiplied by the x values for each individual observation and the resulting products are summed. If the discriminant function has detected differences between the groups, one group will have scores tending toward the high end of the array and the other group will have scores tending toward the low end. The signs of the discriminant coefficients are used to determine the direction of the difference between the two groups.

Because all affiliate banks in the study were acquired over a five-year period, it was necessary for time series–related analysis purposes to collapse all acquisition years to a common point (year 0) representing the year of acquisition. Discriminant model classifications then were conducted cross sectionally, one to three years before acquisition and one to four and, where possible, five to eight years after acquisition by an MBHC. This approach allows for examination of trends or changes over time in financial performance profiles. It also provides for possible insight into whether a specific length of time is necessary for the two groups of banks to perform differently.

Step 4. Using the correlation matrix and the factor loadings produced in step 3, several sets of variables were constructed for subsequent testing. Individual performance variables that did not have high factor loading on any of the principal components were not included in these sets since PCA analysis did not identify these variables as having any discrimination potential between these two groups of banks. An attempt was made not to place any performance variable that was highly correlated with another variable together in any one set of variables.

For each set of variables a discriminant function was constructed, and this discriminant function was used to classify the banks in the same manner as step 3. The results of these classification tests were compared to the results obtained in step 3. The set of variables which appeared to produce the most proficient discriminant function for classification purposes and which could be interpreted for analysis purposes was selected for further multivariate testing.

Step 5. The last phase of Model 1 focused on an analysis of financial performance by group during specific calendar years. This cross-sectional approach permitted the examination of performance differences associated with particular economic conditions and/or monetary policies. Thus, by also examining performance profiles in specific years, it was possible to develop some insight into performance differences that were acquisition-related versus economic or monetary policy related.

Model 2

Identification of performance differences. Model 1 analyzed several performance variables to determine what, if any, performance differences did appear and over what time period they appeared. Next, all banks and subsequently banks grouped together by year of acquisition were examined to ascertain what specific performance variables were most significant in accounting for performance differences. Stepwise discriminant analysis (SDA) was used to identify what specific performance differences did exist in selected test periods. Statistical Package for the Social Science (SPSS) computer programs were used to conduct the SDA analysis.

SDA effectively selects the single best discriminating variable from a set of variables according to a predetermined criterion. Several different criteria may be used to assist in the variable selection process. A second discriminating variable is selected as the variable best able to improve the value of the discrimination criterion in combination with the first variable. The third and subsequent variables are similarly selected according to their ability to contribute to further discrimination. At each step, variables already selected may be removed if they are found to reduce discrimination when combined with more recently selected variables. Eventually, either all the variables will be selected or it will be found that the remaining variables are no longer able to contribute to further discrimination.

Using the set of performance variables identified in Model 1, SDA was used to identify those specific performance variables and independent banks. In this manner any performance differentials were identified. Statistical testing procedures were conducted to determine how statistically significant these differentials were.

Step 1. Using the set of performance variables that resulted from Model 1, SDA was conducted on all banks. Once again it was necessary to collapse all acquisition years to a common point (year 0) representing the year a particular bank was acquired. The categorical dependent variable was given a value of 0 for acquired banks and 1 for independent banks. For all banks and then for each set of banks, SDA was conducted cross-sectionally one to three years before acquisition and one to five and, where possible, six to eight years after acquisition. This cross-sectional approach is quite similar to the profile analysis procedure commonly used in conjunction with analysis of variance testing procedures. The principal difference is that profile analysis tests for equality between two groups, while this model tests for differences between two groups. This approach also permits the existence of differences over time. In this way it is possible to determine what differences did exist at a particular point in time as well as whether or not these differences persisted over time or were subsequently eroded by competitive and market forces. For example, for banks acquired in 1968 SDA was conducted using the year-end financial observations of 1965–67 and 1969–77. A diagram of this cross-sectional analysis appears in figure 3-3.

Figure 3-3 defines the acquisition periods used to compare acquired and independent banks. Table 3-7 highlights the specific SDA tests conducted for each set of banks.

Once the various before and after analyses had been conducted, SDA was run on all banks during specific calendar years. This made it possible to examine what possible effects different economic conditions and/or monetary policies might have on any performance differences between the two groups of banks.

The SPSS computer output for each SDA test consisted of:

1. The group means and group standard deviations for each performance variable
2. The pooled within group covariance matrix

Figure 3-3.   Acquisition Periods Defined

Table 3-7.   SDA Test Years

Year of Acquisition	Preacquisition	Postacquisition
1968	1965–67	1969–77
1969	1966–68	1970–77
1970	1967–69	1971–77
1971	1968–70	1972–77
1972	1969–71	1973–77

3. The pooled within group correlation matrix
4. The results of a one-way analysis of variance test on each discriminating variable, which included the computed Wilks' Lambda, the univariate F-ratio, and the level of significance
5. Total covariance matrix
6. The discriminant function coefficients
7. The discriminant Z scores
8. The classification results
9. The step-by-step results of the SDA

In order to evaluate the classification results of each SDA run, the total efficiency classification statistic Z, used in Model 1, was again calculated. The sign of the discriminant coefficients was examined to determine the direction of the difference between the two groups, and the sizes of the standardized discriminant coefficients and the change in the RAO V statistic for each variable were used to determine their statistical significance.

Step 2. SDA then was conducted on all banks of a common size category. It was necessary for time series–related analysis purposes to collapse all withdrawal years down to a common point (year 0) representing the year of acquisition. SDA was conducted on each size category in the same manner as in step 1. This permitted an examination of any trends or changes over time in financial performance profiles by the five different size categories of banks.

Step 3. Using SAS computer programs, simple descriptive statistics were computed for each individual performance variable for each set of banks on which SDA was conducted. The means, standard deviations, ranges, and high and low values of each performance variable were computed for each set of banks for each test period. These statistics were used to highlight the magnitude of any specific performance differences highlighted by the SDA.

The completion of this phase of the analysis concludes the research design. Table 3-8 reviews each step of the design and related it to each specific research objective.

Summary

In this chapter, a research design and multivariate methodology is established for use in the statistical analysis of the study's objectives and hypotheses. Initially, the data base and performance variables were defined. Next, a research design was formulated and the statistical techniques used in the development of two multivariate models were described.

The objectives of the study and the research design were developed in order to overcome the previously cited shortcomings of earlier MBHC performance studies. The research methodology is offered as a logical and systematic approach for overcoming these shortcomings and statistically testing the research hypotheses.

Table 3-8. Design Steps and Relationship with Research Objectives

Steps in Research Design	Purpose of the Step	Research Objective
Model 1 Step 1: Perform PCA Step 2: Selection of principal components to retain for MDA Step 3: Conduct MDA Step 4: Develop alternate discriminant functions and conduct MDA classification procedures Step 5: Conduct MDA classification procedures on calendar year basis	Data reduction Interpretation of new performance variables Build discriminant function Test for the ability to detect differences and determine over what time periods they appear	*Objective 1:* To determine if MBHC affiliation has a significant impact on the performance of a commercial bank *Objective 3:* To determine over what time period any observed differences occur
Model 2 Step 1: Perform SDA on various sets of banks Step 2: Conduct SDA on banks in various size categories Step 3: Compute descriptive statistics	Identify specific performance differences over time Identify specific performance differences over time Examine the magnitude of any performance differences that exist	*Objective 2:* To determine which available performance measures best discriminate between MBHC and independent bank performance *Objective 3:* To determine over what time period any observed performance differences occur

4

Empirical Results

This chapter presents the results of the empirical analysis. It is organized so that each section coincides with the development of the research design. Initially, the results of the various multivariate applications performed in conjunction with Model 1 are presented. This is followed by the findings associated with Model 2. The results of both models then are related to the hypotheses established in chapter 3 and a determination is made if any or all of these hypotheses must be rejected. Finally, a summary of the study's findings concludes the chapter.

With respect to Model 1, the results of the initial PCA and the subsequent selection and interpretation of these principal components are presented. Using these principal components, a discriminant function is defined and the initial classification results of the MDA are highlighted. The procedure used to develop and analyze additional discriminant functions is developed with the final results of this analysis being summarized. All classification results associated with the final discriminant model then are presented.

For Model 2 the results of the various SDA applications on various sets of banks are presented. This is followed by a review of the SDA procedures that were applied to the five separate size categories of banks included in this study.

Model 1

Initial PCA Results

Using year-end 1977 performance variables for all 310 commercial banks, PCA was used to decrease the performance data to a reduced set of components with as little loss of information as possible. Each of the procedures offered by Green for determining how many principal components to retain for further analysis was examined (Green, 1978). The two primary objectives for factor analyzing the data were to gain an appreciation for the operational significance of the data and to interpret the new principal components or financial dimensions of the data. Therefore, the decision on the number of principal components to extract was determined jointly by the amount of variance explained by each additional principal component and by the interpretability of each principal component. The results of the PCA are summarized in table 4-1. The results indicate that the first eight principal components or factors explain 71.2 percent of the total variance contained in the data set. The inclusion of any additional principal components explained little additional variance and were difficult to interpret.

Table 4-2 summarizes the factor loadings of each performance variable that loaded on each of the eight factors. An analysis of the individual factor loadings for each component suggests that the first factor was a joint measure of asset composition, liquidity, and investing policy. Only ratios containing balance sheet data produced high factor loadings. The second factor indicates that measures of pricing, expense control, and loan composition load very heavily, while the third factor dealt primarily with profitability. In contrast to the first factor, ratios included in factors two and three contained both balance sheet and income statement data. The fourth factor represents specific aspects of asset utilization which are

Table 4-1.   Principal Components Analysis Results Using 76
Performance Variables

Principal Component	Eigenvalue	Portion of Total Variance Explained	Cumulative Portion of Total Variance Explained
1	14.985	.197	.197
2	11.644	.153	.350
3	8.513	.112	.462
4	6.084	.080	.542
5	4.214	.055	.598
6	3.375	.044	.642
7	2.747	.036	.678
8	2.556	.034	.712
9	2.301	.030	.742
10	2.054	.027	.769
11	1.760	.023	.793
12	1.480	.019	.812
13	1.442	.019	.831
14	1.352	.018	.849
15	1.222	.015	.864

Table 4-2. Factor Patterns for Financial Performance
(76 Performance Variables)

Performance Variables				Factor Loadings				
	F_1	F_2	F_3	F_4	F_5	F_6	F_7	F_8
U.S. GOVT. SEC.+U.S. AGN. SEC./TOT. DEP. (R48)	.9335							
U.S. GOVT. SEC.+U.S. AGN. SEC./TOT. ASSETS (R8)	.9294							
LIQ. ASSETS/TOT. ASSETS (R1)	.8958							
LIQ. ASSETS/TOT. DEP. (R27)	.8831							
RISK ASSETS/TOT. ASSETS (R2)	-.8571							
INT. REC'D ON INV./TOT. OPG. INCOME (R49)	.8227							
U.S. GOVT. SEC.+U.S. AGN. SEC.+MUNI. SEC./TOT. DEP. (R44)	.8085							
TOT. LOANS/TOT. DEP. (R11)	-.8053							
U.S. GOVT. SEC./TOT. DEP. (R46)	.8052							
U.S. GOVT. SEC./TOT. ASSETS (R5)	.8040							
TOT. LOANS/TOT. ASSETS (R3)	-.7977							
CASH+U.S. GOVT. SEC./TOT. DEP. (R26)	.7488							
TOT. CAPITAL ACCTS/RISK ASSETS (R39)	.7173							
EQUITY CAPITAL/RISK ASSETS (R35)	.7114							
LIQ. ASSETS/TOT. DEMAND DEP. (R28)	.6789							
TOT. CAPITAL, ACCTS./TOT. LOANS (R41)	.6720							
EQUITY CAPITAL/TOT. LOANS (R37)	.6681							

Performance Variables	F₁	F₂	F₃	F₄	F₅	F₆	F₇	F₈

Factor Loadings

Performance Variables	F_1	F_2	F_3	F_4	F_5	F_6	F_7	F_8
CASH + U.S. GOVT. SEC./DEMAND DEP., IPC (R25)	.6022							
OTHER ORG EXPENSE/TOT. ASSETS (R60)		.7447						
SERVICE CHGS ON DEP./TOT. DEP. (R54)		.7027						
SERVICE CHGS ON DEP./DEMAND DEP., IPC (R50)		.6769						
TOTAL SAL. & BENE./TOT. ASSETS (R63)		.6469						
REAL ESTATE LOANS/TOT. LOANS (R17)		−.6275						
REAL ESTATE LOANS/TOT. ASSETS (R13)		−.6174						
OTHER OPG. EXP./TOT. OPG. EXP. (R61)		.6095						
NET OPG. INCOME/TOT. ASSETS (R65)			.9310					
TOT. OPG. EXP./TOT. ASSETS (R57)			−.9251					
NET INCOME/TOT. ASSETS (R65)			.9080					
NET INCOME/TOT. OPG. INCOME (R69)			.8770					
NET INCOME/TOT. EQUITY CAPITAL (R66)			.8608					
NET OPG. INCOME/TOT. EQUITY CAPITAL (R68)			.8600					
CASH/TOT. ASSETS (R4)				−.8800				
CASH/TOT. DEP. (R24)				−.8797				
EARN. ASSETS/TOT. ASSETS (R10)				.8774				

	Factor 1	Factor 2	Factor 3	Factor 4	Factor 5	Factor 6
EARN. ASSETS/AVAIL. FUNDS (R45)	.8652					
EARN. ASSETS/TOT. DEP. (R22)	.8166					
TOT. CAPITAL ACCTS./TOT. ASSETS (R38)		.8417				
TOT. CAPITAL ACCTS./TOT. DEP. (R40)		.8386				
EQUITY CAPITAL/TOT. DEP. (R36)		.8313				
EQUITY CAPITAL/TOT. ASSETS (R34)		.8255				
CAPITAL+SURPLUS/TOT. DEP. (R43)		.7456				
SURPLUS/TOT. DEP. (R42)		.7397				
GROWTH IN TOT. ASSETS (G70)			.8647			
GROWTH IN TOT. DEP. (G71)			.8611			
GROWTH IN TOT. DEMAND DEP. (G72)			.6283			
CONSUMER LOANS/TOT. LOANS (R20)				.8431		
CONSUMER LOANS/TOT. ASSETS (R12)					.8214	
AUTO LOANS/TOT. LOANS (R21)					.8184	
AUTO LOANS/TOT. ASSETS (R16)					.8010	
MUNI. SEC./TOT. ASSETS (R47)						.6370
MUNI. SEC./TOT. DEP. (R31)						.6318

Note: Only factor loadings of .60 or higher are shown.

measured in terms of both total assets and total deposits. The fifth factor is a measure of capital management. The sixth factor is a measure of growth, the seventh is a measure of consumer lending, and the eighth factor represents that portion of investing policy which relates to the purchase of municipal securities.

No single performance variable appeared in any more than one of the eight factors or dimensions of performance. An analysis of the eight factors revealed that each contained some performance measures that were highly correlated with each other. This suggested that the total number of performance measures that were initially defined should be reduced further before any stepwise discriminant procedures are conducted.

Initial Multiple Discriminant Function Defined

The eight principal component weights then were used to define an eight-variable discriminant function. This was done so that an MDA procedure could be used to test for possible differences and changes in financial performance profiles between affiliate and independent banks.

Because the affiliate banks in the study were acquired by MBHCs over a five-year period, it was necessary for time series–related analysis purposes to collapse all acquisition years down to a common point (YRO) representing the year of acquisition. Discriminant model classifications then were conducted on a cross-section basis for one, two, and three years before acquisition, and one through four, and where possible five to eight, years after acquisition by a MBHC. This cross-section approach permits the examinations of trends or changes over time in financial performance profiles. It also provides for some insight into what length of time is necessary for the acquired banks to adjust to their holding company status.

Each bank was classified into the affiliate or independent group categories on the basis of its discriminant "Z" score. The model for classifying a bank utilized the eight derived principal component weights and the linearized discriminant functions used in the model appear in figure 4-1. It was postulated that if performance profile differences did, in fact, occur over time between banks that were acquired by MBHCs and banks that remained independent of MBHCs, the classification capabilities should change accordingly.

Table 4-3 contains the results of the classification procedures over time for one through three years before acquisition and for one through eight years (where possible) after acquisition. This approach permits the analysis of possible performance profile differences within the context of a time series framework. Using a total efficiency measure developed for

Figure 4-1.   Linearized Discriminant Functions
(Eight Factors)

Acquired Banks: $Z = -.054 - .244 F_1 + .055 F_2 + .023 F_3 + .052 F_4 + .052 F_5 - .108 F_6$
$+ .142 F_7 + .137 F_8$

Independent Banks: $Z = -.050 + .236 F_1 - .053 F_2 - .022 F_3 - .050 F_4 - .049 F_5 + .104 F_6$
$- .137 F_7 - .132 F_8$

financial applications of discriminant analysis, the statistical significance of each classification procedure was determined (Joy and Tollefson, 1975). This table highlights several interesting results. All but one of the postacquisition years is characterized by total classification percentages which are significantly different from a chance classification at the .05 level. The remaining one is significantly different from a chance classification at the .10 level. However, the three preacquisition periods have total classifications approximately equal to the expected chance classification of 50 percent. This implies that both the affiliate and independent groups were similar in nature, relative to the discriminant model, during the period prior to which the affiliate banks were acquired by MBHCs. The data also reveal that an initial improvement in the classification percentages takes place immediately (YR+1) after the banks were acquired by various MBHCs. This improvement continues to increase through year three, and then it stays relatively constant for an additional three years before declining slightly. This suggests that any performance differences between the two groups do appear almost immediately, but a MBHC acquisition does not become a "seasoned" affiliate until somewhere between three and five to six years after its acquisition.

An examination of the individual group classification adds additional insight into the nature of the preacquisition and postacquisition periods. In the preacquisition period, the discriminant function tended to classify the independent banks more effectively than the affiliate groups. The classifications also indicate that a substantial portion of the affiliate group had characteristics similar to independent banks and to such an extent that they were misclassified. The analysis also shows that in the preacquisition period and in the very early stages of the post-acquisition period (YR+1 and YR+2) that most of the banks maintained the profile of independent banks as depicted by the discriminant function. As time progressed after acquisition, the affiliate banks began to take on more of the characteristics that were common to them in 1977. In addition the independent banks began to take on attributes similar to those possessed by the affiliate group. By the fifth year the discriminant function was able to classify only 56 percent of the independent banks correctly. It appears

Table 4-3. MDA Classification of Acquired and Independent Banks before and after Acquisition Using a 76-variable Set

Correctly Classified	Preacquisition Period			Postacquisition Period						
	YR-3	YR-2	YR-1	YR+1	YR+2	YR+3	YR+4	YR+5	YR+6	YR+7
Acquired Bank Group										
Number	26	29	34	68	88	103	100	81	59	26
Percent	(16.7)	(18.7)	(21.9)	(43.9)	(56.7)	(66.5)	(64.5)	(64.8)	(72.8)	(74.2)
Independent Bank Group										
Number	131	127	119	105	90	88	88	70	33	15
Percent	(84.5)	(81.9)	(76.7)	(67.7)	(58.1)	(56.7)	(56.7)	(56.0)	(40.7)	(42.8)
Total Bank Group										
Number	157	156	153	173	178	191	188	151	92	41
Percent	(50.6)	(50.3)	(49.3)	(55.8)**	(57.4)*	(61.6)*	(60.6)*	(60.4)*	(56.7)*	(58.5)*

*Significantly different from a chance classification at the .05 level.
**Significantly different from a chance classification at the .10 level.

Note: Table shows number, with percentages in parentheses, of each group that was correctly classified. Each year was based on 310 observations with the following exceptions: YR+5 (250 observations), YR+6 (162 observations), YR+7 (70 observations).

from the data provided by the classification procedures that several years elapsed before the affiliate group was able to attain the profile they possessed in 1977. The results further indicate that independent banks also seem to have adjusted over time and began to take on more of the attributes associated with the affiliate group.

Further Data Reduction

The factor loadings identified in table 4-2 suggested that several of the performance variables were highly correlated with one another. Using the covariance matrix portion of the SAS output, these variables were identified. Individual performance variables that did not have a high factor loading greater than .50 on any of the eight principal components were removed from the original list of 76 performance variables. Then various sets of variables were assembled such that, when possible, those variables that were highly correlated with each were not placed in the same set. In addition, some preference was given to including those variables that had consistently been identified in earlier univariate and multivariate studies as having high discriminatory power in differentiating between affiliate and independent banks. This procedure attempted to make maximum use of all available information so as to minimize the possibility of overlooking important performance profile characteristics. The final selection of the set of variables that would be used for further testing and analysis contained only those performance variables that either were identified statistically as having some discriminating power to correctly classify the banks included in this study or were identified in earlier studies as having this capability.

Final Multiple Discriminant Function Defined

Each of the eight sets of performance variables was subjected to the discriminant model classification scheme described earlier. The results were compared and the set of 28 performance variables was retained for further analysis. This particular set of variables possessed the best discriminating power of all sets tested, and its principal components could be interpreted. Those performance variables included in this group are listed in figure 4-2.

Once again a PCA analysis was conducted using the year-end 1977 performance variables for all 310 commercial banks. Table 4-4 summarizes the results of the PCA. Using the same retention criteria specified earlier, seven principal components were retained which explained 78.4 percent of the total variance contained in the data set.

Figure 4-2.   Performance Variables Selected for Further Testing

1. U.S. Government Securities/Total Assets (R5)
2. Earning Assets***/Total Assets (R10)
3. Total Loans/Total Deposits (R11)
4. Real Estate Loans/Total Loans (R17)
5. Commercial and Industrial Loans/Total Loans (R18)
6. Consumer Loans/Total Loans (R20)
7. Liquid Assets*/Total Deposits (R27)
8. Liquid Assets*/Total Demand Deposits (R28)
9. Deposits of State and Political Subdivisions/Total Deposits (R31)
10. Total Time Deposits/Total Deposits (R33)
11. Total Capital Accounts/Total Assets (R38)
12. Total Capital Accounts/Risk Assets** (R39)
13. Total Capital Accounts/Total Loans (R41)
14. U.S. Government Securities + U.S. Government Agency Securities + State and Political Subdivision Securities/Total Deposits (R44)
15. Earning Assets***/Available Funds**** (R45)
16. Interest Received on Investments/Total Operating Income (R49)
17. Total Service Charges and Fees/Total Operating Income (R53)
18. Service Charges on Deposits/Total Deposits (R54)
19. (Interest and Fee on Loans/Total Loan) – (Interest on Deposits)/(Total Time and Savings Deposits) (R55)
20. Total Operating Expense/Total Assets (R57)
21. Total Operating Expense/Total Operating Income (R59)
22. Other Operating Expense/Total Assets (R60)
23. Other Operating Expense/Total Operating Expense (R61)
24. Total Salaries + Employee Benefits/Total Assets (R63)
25. Net Income/Total Assets (R65)
26. Net Income/Total Equity Capital (R66)
27. Growth in Total Assets (R70)
28. Growth in Total Capital Accounts (R76)

*Liquid Assets = Cash and Due + U.S. Government Securities + U.S. Agency Securities + Federal Funds Sold
**Risk Assets = Obligations of State and Political Subdivisions + Other Securities Held + Total Loans + Other Assets
***Earning Assets = All Securities Held + Total Loans
****Available Funds = Total Deposits + Federal Funds Purchased

Table 4-5 summarizes the factor loadings of the various performance variables that loaded on each of the seven factors. An analysis of the individual factor loadings for each component suggested that the first factor was a measure of investing policy and capital management. The second factor was primarily a factor of expense control while the third factor measured profitability. The fourth factor was a measure of asset utilization, the fifth factor a measure of growth, and the sixth factor a measure of loan composition. The seventh factor represented a specific aspect of investing policy. Once again no single performance variable possessed a significant factor loading (greater than .60) on any more than one of the seven factors or dimensions of performance. However, none

Table 4-4. Principal Components Analysis Results Using 28
Performance Variables

Principal Component	Eigenvalue	Portion of Total Variance Explained	Cumulative Portion of Total Variance Explained
1	6.738	.241	.241
2	5.435	.194	.435
3	3.375	.121	.555
4	2.538	.091	.646
5	1.616	.058	.704
6	1.166	.042	.745
7	1.071	.038	.784
8	.956	.034	.818
9	.869	.031	.849
10	.681	.024	.873

of the seven factors contained more than a few performance variables that were highly correlated with each other. To this extent the level of multicollinearity in these seven factors was significantly smaller relative to the eight-factor model developed earlier.

A comparison of the seven principal components which were extracted from the 28 performance variable set revealed that they highlighted similar performance dimensions to the eight principal components obtained from the 76 variables originally identified in this study. In addition to reducing the level of correlation among the variables, this additional data reduction procedure produced a smaller set of 28 variables which explained about 7 percent more the total variance of the data set. The components were easier to interpret after the reduction of the number of performance variables.

The seven principal components' weights then were used to define a seven-variable discriminant function. Using the classification procedure discussed earlier, this discriminant function was used to test for possible differences and changes in financial performance profiles between affiliate and independent banks. The discriminant model used to classify the banks is defined in figure 4-3.

First Phase: Classification Analysis

Table 4-6 summarizes the classification results. The results are very similar to those described in table 4-3. In all but one of the postacquisition

Table 4-5.   Factor Patterns for Financial Performance
(28 Performance Variables)

Performance Variables	Factor Loadings						
	F_1	F_2	F_3	F_4	F_5	F_6	F_7
INT. REC'D ON INV./TOT. OPG. INCOME (R49)	.8882						
U.S. GOVT. SEC. + U.S. AGN. SEC. + MUNI. SEC./TOT. DEP. (R44)	.8805						
TOT. LOANS/TOT. DEP. (R11)	-.8386						
LIQ. ASSETS/TOT. DEP. (R27)	.8199						
TOT. CAPITAL ACCTS./TOT. LOANS (R41)	.7930						
TOT. CAPITAL ACCTS./RISK ASSETS (R35)	.7919						
U.S. GOVT. SEC./TOT. ASSETS (R5)	.7666						
OTHER OPG. EXPEN./TOT. ASSETS (R60)		.8522					
OTHER OPG. EXPEN./TOT. OP. INCOME (R59)		.8122					
SERVICE CHGS ON DEP./TOT. DEP. (R54)		.8100					
TOT. SERVICE CHGS AND FEES/TOT. OPG. INCOME (R53)		.7965					
TOT. SAL. & BENE./TOT. ASSETS (R63)		.7444					
CONSUMER LOANS/TOT. LOANS (R20)		.6803					
NET INCOME/TOT. ASSETS (R65)			.9493				
TOT. OPG. EXPEN./TOT. OPG. INCOME (R59)			.9213				

	Factor 1	Factor 2	Factor 3	Factor 4	Factor 5
NET INCOME/TOT. EQUITY CAPITAL (R66)	.8171				
EARN. ASSETS/AVAIL. FUNDS (R45)		.9362			
GROWTH IN TOT. ASSETS (G70)			.7164		
GROWTH IN TOT. CAPITAL ACCTS. (G76)			.7040		
TOT. CAPITAL ACCTS./TOT. ASSETS (R38)			−.6466		
COMM. + INDUSTRIAL LOANS/TOT. LOANS (R18)				−.8398	
REAL ESTATE LOANS/TOTAL LOANS (R17)				.6983	
MUNI. DEP./TOTAL DEP. (R31)					.7955

Note: Only factor loadings of .60 or higher are shown.

Figure 4-3.   Linearized Discriminant Functions
(Seven Factors)

Acquired Banks: $Z = -.049 - .227\,F_1 + .117\,F_2 + .072\,F_3 + .050\,F_4 - .182\,F_5 + .035\,F_6$
$- .014\,F_7$

Independent Banks: $Z = -.046 + .219\,F_1 - .113\,F_2 - .069\,F_3 - .048\,F_4 + .176\,F_5 - .034\,F_6$
$- .014\,F_7$

years the results are characterized by total classification percentages which are significantly different from a chance classification at the .05 level. The remaining year is significantly different from a chance classification at the .10 level. The three preacquisition periods have total classifications approximately equal to the expected chance classification of 50 percent. This confirms the previous implication that both the affiliate and independent groups were similar in nature, relative to the discriminant model, during the period prior to which the affiliate banks were acquired by MBHCs. The data reveal that the initial improvement in the classification results takes place immediately after the banks were acquired. The improvement continues to increase through year three, and then it stays relatively constant for the remaining five years although there is a very small decrease in years four and five. In fact the only noticeable difference between these classification results and those discussed earlier is that a small drop in classification percentages occurs in YR+5 as opposed to YR+6.

The individual group classification results confirm what was noted earlier. In the preacquisition period, the discriminant function tended to classify the independent banks more effectively than the affiliate banks. As time progressed after acquisition, the affiliate banks began to take on more of the characteristics that were common to them in 1977. The independent banks also began to take on attributes similar to those possessed by the affiliate group. Once again the independent banks seem to have adjusted over time and began to take on more of the attributes associated with the affiliate banks.

Second Phase: Classification Analysis

A second phase of the aggregate classification model analysis which was conducted focused on financial performance by group during specific calendar years. This permits the examination of performance differences associated with particular economic conditions and monetary policies and makes it possible to develop some insight into performance differences that were acquisition-related versus economic or monetary policy-related.

Table 4-6. MDA Classification of Acquired and Independent Banks before and after Acquisition Using a 28-variable Set

Correctly Classified	Preacquisition Period			Postacquisition Period						
	YR-3	YR-2	YR-1	YR+1	YR+2	YR+3	YR+4	YR+5	YR+6	YR+7
Acquired Bank Group										
Number	39	44	47	65	76	101	107	81	60	26
Percent	(25.2)	(28.4)	(30.3)	(41.9)	(49.0)	(65.2)	(69.0)	(64.8)	(74.1)	(74.3)
Independent Bank Group										
Number	117	106	107	103	99	96	82	68	42	18
Percent	(75.4)	(68.3)	(69.0)	(66.4)	(63.8)	(61.9)	(52.9)	(54.9)	(51.8)	(51.4)
Total Bank Group										
Number	156	150	154	168	175	197	189	149	102	44
Percent	(50.3)	(48.3)	(49.6)	(54.2)**	(56.4)*	(63.5)*	(60.9)*	(59.6)*	(62.9)*	(62.9)*

*Significantly different from a chance classification at the .05 level.
**Significantly different from a chance classification at the .10 level.
Note: Table shows number, with percentages in parentheses, of each group that was correctly classified. Each year was based on 310 observations with the following exceptions: YR+5 (250 observations), YR+6 (162 observations), YR+7 (70 observations).

In this phase of the analysis no attempt was made to identify a particular pre- or postacquisition interval. The results of the classification are presented in table 4-7.

When compared to the affiliate and independent bank group classification schemes highlighted in table 4-6, the data illustrate that the 1969–70 and 1973–74 periods appear to have had a significant impact on the nature of the banks comprising both these groups. Both of these periods were periods of restrictive monetary policy and tight money conditions. This is demonstrated by the substantial change in the discriminant model's ability to classify correctly the overall sample into the appropriate groupings.

In this case the general trend associated with each group classification that was displayed in table 4-6 did not appear. Instead correct classifications of the affiliate banks increased from 20.0 to 40.0 percent from 1969 to 1970 and then fell to 29.6 percent in 1971. From 1973 to 1974 the percent correctly classified rose from 55.5 to 78.1 percent. For the independent banks the percentage changes were from 90.0 to 62.9 percent for 1969 to 1970 and 60.0 to 48.2 percent from 1973 to 1974. Based on the tightness of monetary policy during these time periods and the subsequent pattern of classifications around these periods, it seems that a severe reduction in the money supply and/or other monetary aggregates influenced the performance of both affiliate and independent banks in a similar fashion. Its results imply that severe monetary and economic conditions do have a significant impact on commercial bank performance. In this situation the impact is so great that it seems to override some of the apparent affects of MBHC affiliation on bank performance. Stated differently, it appears that the existence of possible alternate management philosophies related to MBHC affiliation are somewhat neutralized by tight monetary conditions.

Model 2

First Phase: SDA Analysis

In Model 2 SDA was employed to isolate which of the 28 performance variables accounted for the major performance differences between the two groups of banks. Due to the large number of potential candidates in each time period, some degree of instability existed from year to year in variables entering the discriminant function. To facilitate the analysis only those variables which accounted for a significant change in the RAO V statistic[1] and which appeared in at least three or more of the functions in either or both the time series and the time period analyses were consid-

Table 4-7. MDA Classification of Acquired and Independent Banks before and after Acquisition Using a 28-variable Set by Calendar Year

Correctly Classified	Calendar Year							
	1969	1970	1971	1972	1973	1974	1975	1976
				Acquired Bank Group				
Number	2	14	24	47	86	121	94	103
Percent	(20.0)	(40.0)	(29.6)	(37.6)	(55.5)	(78.1)	(60.6)	(66.4)
				Independent Bank Group				
Number	9	22	62	95	93	75	95	88
Percent	(90.0)	(62.9)	(76.5)	(76.0)	(60.0)	(48.3)	(61.2)	(56.8)
				Total Bank Group				
Number	11	36	86	142	179	196	189	191
Percent	(55.0)	(51.4)	(53.1)	(56.8)**	(57.7)**	(63.2)*	(61.0)*	(61.6)*

*Significantly different from a chance classification at the .05 level.
**Significantly different from a chance classification at the .10 level.

Note: Table shows number, with percentages in parentheses, of each group that was correctly classified. Each year was based on 310 observations with the following exceptions: 1969 (10 observations), 1970 (70 observations), 1971 (162 observations), and 1972 (250 observations).

ered to be important discriminators between the affiliate and independent bank groups. Of the 28 possible entrants, 10 met the selection criteria. These 10 performance variables appear in table 4-8. The table highlights each variable's cross-sectional significance over time both before and after acquisition.

The ratio of U.S. government securities to total assets was the most consistent variable appearing in every period except YR-2. An examination of the variable's mean values indicates that independent banks consistently held a higher percentage of U.S. government securities than their affiliate bank counterparts. This difference appeared in both the preacquisition and postacquisition periods. This suggests that MBHC affiliation had little affect over time on the percentage of U.S. government securities that either group held. However, the examination of the variable's group means indicated that affiliate banks did appear to decrease their relative holdings of U.S. government securities somewhat after their acquisition. Given the ability of this item to discriminate between the two groups in both periods, it was concluded that this performance trait was not greatly affected by MBHC affiliation. It is also interesting to note the relative importance of this variable in each year based on the size of its standardized discriminant coefficient. In six of the nine years that it entered the discriminant function its relative weight was sixth or higher. This indicates that although this variable is a statistically significant discriminator, it is not as significant relative to many other of the performance variables identified in table 4-8.

Another measure of investing policy which met the criteria for entering the discriminant function was the ratio of U.S. government securities + U.S. government agency securities + municipal securities to total deposits. The results indicated that the independent banks invested a higher percentage in these types of marketable securities than the affiliate banks. In this case the variable means revealed that prior to acquisition there was relatively little difference between the two groups. However, almost immediately after acquisition the independent banks began to hold a higher percentage of these securities. This difference was most significant in periods YR+4, YR+5, and YR+6. Since U.S. government securities are a major component of this ratio, it is no surprise that these two investing policy ratios reflect similar differences in performance. It seems apparent that independent banks had a slight preference for larger investment portfolios relative to both its asset and deposit bases.

A review of the two ratios which incorporate earning assets in their numerators, earning assets to total assets and earning assets to available funds, indicates that once acquired an affiliate bank ultimately achieved higher asset utilization ratios than the independent banks. Both ratios had

Table 4-8. Significant Variables Entering the Stepwise Discriminant Function by before and after Acquisition Period Using a 28-variable Set

Variable	YR−3	YR−2	YR−1	YR+1	YR+2	YR+3	YR+4	YR+5	YR+6	YR+7
U.S. GOVT. SEC./TOT. ASSETS (R5)	6a	2a	8b		3a	7a	10b	7a	10a	2a
EARN. ASSETS/TOT. ASSETS (R10)					2a	2a		3a	3a	5a
TOT. LOANS/TOT. DEP. (R11)	1b					3a		2a	2a	
TOT. TIME DEP./TOT. DEP. (R33)		3b			4a		5b		6a	8b
TOT. CAPITAL ACCTS./TOT. LOANS (R41)		1a							4a	
U.S. GOVT. SEC. + U.S. GOVT. AGN. SEC. + MUNI. SEC./TOT. DEP. (R44)	4a				1a	1b	4b	1b	1a	
EARN. ASSETS/AVAIL. FUNDS (R45)							2a			
OTHER OPG. EXPENSE/TOT. OPG. EXPENSE (R61)	5b					6a	6b			1a
NET INCOME/TOT. EQUITY CAPITAL (R66)								10b	5a	4a
GROWTH IN TOT. CAPITAL ACCOUNTS (G76)									11a	3a

Where the data contained in each cell indicates:

1 thru 11 = Relative importance of variable in each year based on the size of its standardized discriminant coefficient.
a = Variable accounted for a significant change in the RAO V statistic at the .05 level.
b = Variable accounted for a significant change in the RAO V statistic at the .10 level.

relatively high standardized discriminant coefficients and both were statistically significant at the .05 level. In each situation the affiliate banks seemed to achieve these results beginning with the second year after acquisition. However, the earning assets to total assets advantage continued to be significant through YR+7 while the earning assets to available funds advantage seemed to be less apparent after YR+4. In each case it appears that MBHC affiliation did affect the level of asset utilization as early as two years after acquisition. This advantage seemed to be sustained over most of the remaining postacquisition period.

An examination of the asset composition ratios highlighted that affiliate banks appear to have achieved higher total loan-to-deposit ratios than their paired independent bank counterparts. This difference appeared in only one year of the preacquisition period (YR−3) as compared to three years in the postacquisition period. Large relative percentage differences appeared immediately after acquisition and were most significant three to six years after acquisition. The variable's means showed that this percentage difference grew in the first three years after acquisition and then stabilized in subsequent years. This suggests a more aggressive loan posture on behalf of the affiliate banks and an apparent attempt on the affiliate bank's part to expand its loan portfolio after acquisition. This result is consistent with the earlier finding that independent banks had a greater preference for investing their funds in marketable securities.

With regard to deposit structure, the ratio of total time deposits to total deposits appeared in both the preacquisition and postacquisition years. The presence of this variable and an analysis of its group mean values indicate that the affiliate banks were more aggressive in trying to attract more costly, longer-term deposits. This aggressiveness appears to increase later in the postacquisition period. This is consistent with and could serve as a possible means for supporting their increased levels of asset utilization and their higher loan-to-deposit ratios.

In terms of capital structure, the ratio of total capital accounts to total loans indicates that independent banks maintain a higher percentage of capital to total loans. In the preacquisition period this variable entered the discriminant function and the variable means indicated that, at that time, the affiliate banks had the higher ratio of capital to total loans. However, after acquisition this situation was reversed beginning with YR+2. From this point on independent banks maintained the higher ratio of capital to total loans. This suggests that MBHCs displayed a preference for purchasing well-capitalized banks (relative to their independent bank counterparts) and then apparently may have utilized this capital elsewhere within the holding company. This is consistent with the belief that MBHCs may be able to use its collective capital base more efficiently throughout the holding company system. It also indicates that individual MBHC affiliates tend to operate with smaller capital ratios than independent banks.

Relative to expense control, the SDA analysis revealed that affiliate banks had higher ratios of other operating expenses to total operating expense than the independent banks. These differences did not appear in the preacquisition period, but they did begin to appear immediately after acquisition. In fact, prior to acquisition, independent banks had the higher ratio. By YR+4 the differences were rather significant and they continued to increase through YR+7. These results support the argument that holding companies do pass through many of their operating expenses down to their affiliate banks.

In the area of profitability there seems to be no real consistent performance differential favoring either group. In the preacquisition period, the independent banks tended to have higher net income to total equity capital ratios than the affiliate banks. An examination of variable's means reveals that immediately after acquisition the affiliate banks had a slightly higher return on equity ratio but by YR+3 the independent banks had gained a significant edge. For the next three years the two exhibited similar profitability performance. By YR+7 affiliate banks once again displayed higher net income to total equity capital ratios. What is concluded from these results is highly dependent upon the length of the postacquisition period selected. In addition, it must be noted that the magnitudes of the standardized discriminant coefficients are only moderately strong relative to the other performance measures in the discriminant function.

With regards to growth in total capital accounts, the results indicate that independent banks experience a higher growth rate with regards to capital acquisition later on in the postacquisition period. In the preacquisition period, the affiliate banks exhibited greater capital growth. These findings are consistent with earlier findings which indicated that MBHCs tend to utilize less capital in their operation than do independent banks. However, an examination of the standardized discriminant coefficients reveals that this ratio possessed the weakest discriminatory power relative to the other nine variables which have been identified in the various stepwise discriminant functions.

In order to further test for possible performance differences the SDA procedure was applied to the five groups of affiliate and independent banks when segmented by their year of acquisition. Although each subset of the total sample was significantly smaller than the aggregate analysis, the results of the analyses conducted on banks acquired in 1969, 1970, 1971, and 1972 are generally consistent with the aggregate analysis. With only 10 bank pairs in the 1968 acquired subset, the results were too unstable to analyze.

The final step in this phase of the analysis was to run SDA on a cross-sectional basis for specific calendar years using as many of the 310 banks as possible. These results appear in table 4-9. It should be noted at the outset that the individual standardized discriminant coefficient weights are very similar to those which each variable received in table 4-7. Of specific interest is the fact that during 1973 and 1974 very few variables entered the discriminant function when compared to the other time periods. This supports earlier MDA classification results which revealed that tight monetary and economic conditions tended to moderate the differences that existed between the two bank groups. Although not totally identical results were evident in the 1967–70 time period, it must be noted that this period experienced much less restrictive monetary conditions than the 1973–74 time period and the underlying sample size in both those years was not as great as in the 1973–74 period. It is also apparent that many of the differences that did appear between the two groups did so immediately after the tight economic conditions that prevailed during the 1973–74 period had abated. This period also coincides with a time when more of the acquired banks in this study had become more "seasoned" affiliate banks and the holding company affiliation began to have more of an effect on these acquired banks.

Second Phase: SDA Analysis

The second and final phase of Model 2 applied the SDA procedure to subsets of paired banks that had been segmented into five distinct size categories. The purpose of this phase of the analysis was to determine if those differences in financial performance which did exist in previous analyses appeared uniformly over all size categories.

Size category 1. There were 53 paired banks in the total sample that had total assets of less than $10 million. The results of the SDA analysis performed on these banks appears in table 4-10. The results are generally consistent with the results obtained from the same type of analysis previously performed on all 310 banks. However, three additional ratios satisfied the criteria associated with entering the stepwise discriminant function.

Two of the new variables which entered these discriminant functions were loan composition variables. The ratio of commercial and industrial loans to total loans becomes a significant performance variable in the postacquisition period after YR+3. The variable's mean values indicate

Table 4-9. Significant Variables Entering the Stepwise Discriminant Function
by Calendar Year Using a 28-variable Set

Variable	1969	1970	1971	1972	1973	1974	1975	1976	1977
U.S. GOVT. SEC./TOT. ASSETS (R51)	3a	6a	5a		2a	4a	8a	5a	6a
EARN. ASSETS/TOT. ASSETS (R10)					2b		3a	3b	3a
TOT. LOANS/TOT. DEP. (R11)		1b					1a	2a	2a
TOT. TIME DEP./TOT. DEP. (R33)			1b					8b	5a
TOT. CAPITAL ACCTS./TOT. LOANS (R41)		3a							
U.S. GOVT. SEC. + U.S. GOVT. AGN. SEC. + MUNI. SEC./TOT. DEP. (R44)						2a	2a	1a	1a
EARN. ASSETS/AVAIL. FUNDS (R45)	2b	5b		1a					
OTHER OPG. EXPENSE/TOT. OPG. EXPENSE (R61)							5a	4a	4a
NET INCOME/TOT. EQUITY CAPITAL (R66)							9b		9b
GROWTH IN TOT. CAPITAL ACCTS. (G76)		9a							7a

Where the data contained in each cell indicates:

1 thru 9 = Relative importance of variable in each year based on the size of its standardized discriminant coefficient.
      a = Variable accounted for a significant change in the RAO V statistic at the .05 level.
      b = Variable accounted for a significant change in the RAO V statistic at the .10 level.

Table 4-10. Significant Variables Entering the Stepwise Discriminant Function by before and after Acquisition Period
(Size Category 1)

Variable	YR−3	YR−2	YR−1	YR+1	YR+2	YR+3	YR+4	YR+5	YR+6	YR+7
U.S. GOVT. SEC./TOT. ASSETS (R5)	1a			3a	1a	3a	2a	3a	8a	
EARN. ASSETS/TOT. ASSETS (R10)		3b	5b		5b	2b				
TOT. LOANS/TOT. DEP. (R11)						5b				
C+I LOANS/TOT. LOANS (R18)				7a	2b	9b			9a	8a
CONSUMER LOANS/TOT. LOANS (R20)						4b				
TOT. TIME DEP./TOT. DEP. (R33)			4a							
TOT. CAPITAL ACCTS./TOT. LOANS (R38)					3a				4b	5b
TOT. CAPITAL ACCTS./TOT. LOANS (R41)									3a	3b
U.S. GOVT. SEC. + U.S. GOVT. AGN. SEC. + MUNI. SEC./TOT. DEP. (R44)				1a	4a	1b			5a	
EARN. ASSETS/AVAIL. FUNDS (R45)	4b									
OTHER OPG. EXPENSES/TOT. OPG. EXPENSES (R61)				4a	6b			1b	2a	1b
NET INCOME/TOT. EQUITY CAPITAL (R66)										9a
GROWTH IN TOTAL CAPITAL ACCOUNTS (G76)				8a					6a	7b

Where the data contained in each cell indicates:

1 thru 9 = Relative importance of variable in each year based on the size of its standardized discriminant coefficient.

a = Variable accounted for a significant change in the RAO V statistic at the .05 level.

b = Variable accounted for a significant change in the RAO V statistic at the .10 level.

that the independent banks made a higher percentage of commercial and industrial loans than their affiliate bank counterparts. This effectively reversed the trend evident throughout the preacquisition period and the early stages of the postacquisition period when the affiliate banks held a slightly higher percentage of commercial and industrial loans. Coincident to this the SDA results indicate that immediately after acquisition affiliate banks made a smaller percentage of consumer loans to total loans. However, beginning in YR+4 the variable's mean values indicate that the affiliate banks reversed this trend and began to make a higher percentage of consumer loans to total loans than the independent banks. This trend continued to grow throughout the later stages of the postacquisition period. These findings indicate that over time the smallest affiliate banks exhibited a preference for making more consumer loans at the expense of commercial and industrial loans. When considered in conjunction with earlier findings, it appears that small affiliate banks have a tendency to utilize their higher loan-to-deposit ratios to offer more consumer loans in their marketplace relative to their independent bank competitors.

The third variable which appears in this SDA analysis is the ratio of total capital accounts to total assets. The results obtained from analyzing this variable serves to confirm previous findings that later in the postacquisition period independent banks employ more capital relative to total assets than do affiliate banks. Once again the findings suggest that the affiliate banks operate with smaller capital ratios than independent banks.

Size category 2. This subset of banks included 62 matched pairs whose asset size ranged from $11 million to $25 million. The SDA results for this group of banks appears in table 4-11. Only one additional performance variable met the criteria for entering the stepwise discriminant function. None of the three performance variables which appeared in size category one reappeared while the majority of the ten performance variables originally identified in table 4-8 exhibited similar patterns of performance.

The ratio of service charges on deposits to total deposits appeared during one year in the preacquisition period and during two years in the postacquisition period. An examination of the variable's group means revealed that throughout both periods affiliate banks maintained ratios of service charges on deposits to total deposits that were greater than the independent banks. The relative size of the standardized discriminant coefficients was similar for both periods. The fact that this difference appeared in both periods suggests that holding company affiliation did not substantially effect this dimension of performance. However, it does appear from YR+4 on that the differences between the two groups begin to diminish and that by the fifth year after acquisition the affiliate banks

Table 4-11. Significant Variables Entering the Stepwise Discriminant Function
by before and after Acquisition Period
(Size Category 2)

Variable	YR−3	YR−2	YR−1	YR+1	YR+2	YR+3	YR+4	YR+5	YR+6	YR+7
U.S. GOVT. SEC./TOT. ASSETS (R5)	4b	3b	3b							
EARN. ASSETS/TOT. ASSETS (R10)					2a		2b	5b		1a
TOT. LOANS/TOT. DEP. (R11)						3a		2a	6b	
TOT. TIME DEP./TOT. DEP. (R33)							1a	9b		
TOT. CAPITAL ACCTS./TOT. LOANS (R41)			1b	4b						
U.S. GOVT. SEC. + U.S. GOVT. AGN. SEC. + MUNI. SEC./TOT. DEP. (R44)				2b				1b		
EARN. ASSETS/AVAIL. FUNDS (R45)					1a					
SERVICE CHGS. ON DEP./TOT. DEP. (R54)	2b				2a	4a				
OTHER OPG. EXPENSE/TOT. OPG. EXPENSE (R61)							6b	4b		
NET INCOME/TOT. EQUITY CAPITAL (R66)						5a			1b	
GROWTH IN TOT. CAPITAL ACCTS. (G76)					4b	6b			9b	

Where the data contained in each cell indicates:

1 thru 9 = Relative importance of variable in each year based on the size of its standardized discriminant coefficient.
  a = Variable accounted for a significant change in the RAO V statistic at the .05 level.
  b = Variable accounted for a significant change in the RAO V statistic at the .10 level.

and the independent banks have almost identical ratios of service charges on deposits to total deposits. This suggests that over time the two groups become more alike in this financial performance dimension. This could well be in response to the competitive pressures they place on each other in their marketplace.

Two ratios did not exhibit the same performance profiles that appeared in the aggregate analysis. The U.S. government securities/total assets and the U.S. government securities + U.S. government agencies securities + municipal securities ratios reflected different performance profiles. In this size category the independent banks continued to maintain higher ratios for both variables in the preacquisition period. However, in the postacquisition period this difference had less statistical significance. The variable's group means suggest that the relative size of the differences does diminish over time. This suggests that for somewhat larger banks this performance differential is not as great as it was for smaller banks. It should also be noted that neither of the loan composition differences that appeared in size category 1 appeared.

Size Category 3. In the third size category there were 26 matched pairs of banks with assets ranging from $26 million to $50 million. The results of the SDA analysis on this group of banks appears in table 4-12. The results in this table reveal that the loan composition ratios of commercial and industrial loans to total loans and consumer loans to total loans once again did enter the stepwise discriminant function in the postacquisition period. The ratio of total time deposits to total deposits and the ratio of earning assets to available funds did not enter the stepwise discriminant function in any period.

Two new performance variables did appear in this analysis that had not previously appeared in any other SDA analysis. The liquid assets/total deposits ratio appeared in one year in the preacquisition period (YR−2) and in two years of the postacquisition period (YR+2 and YR+3). The variable's group means indicate that the independent banks held higher liquidity than the affiliate banks in each of these periods. This is consistent with earlier findings that affiliate banks had higher loan to deposit ratios. However, after YR+3 these differences began to disappear and by the end of the postacquisition period these differences were very slight and were not statistically significant. This suggests that competitive pressures may have had an effect on the liquidity management policies of both groups of banks.

The expense control dimension of total salaries and employee benefits to total assets entered the discriminant function in the first three years after acquisition. An examination of the standardized discriminant

Table 4-12. Significant Variables Entering the Stepwise Discriminant Function
by before and after Acquisition Period
(Size Category 3)

Variable	YR−3	YR−2	YR−1	YR+1	YR+2	YR+3	YR+4	YR+5	YR+6	YR+7
U.S. GOVT. SEC./TOT. ASSETS (R5)	5b						1a		5b	
EARN. ASSETS/TOT. ASSETS (R10)										2a
TOT. LOANS/TOT. DEP. (R11)		1a			5b	2b	8b			
C + I LOANS/TOT. LOANS (R18)					1a	7a			9b	7a
CONSUMER LOANS/TOT. LOANS (R20)	3a	5b			7a	3a	4b		7a	5a
LIQ. ASSETS/TOT. DEP. (R27)		2b			2b	8b				
TOT. CAPITAL ACCTS./TOT. LOANS (R41)	1b							6a		3a
U.S. GOVT. SEC. + U.S. GOVT. AGN. SEC. + MUNI. SEC./TOT. DEP. (R45)	6a								4b	
OTHER OPG. EXPENSE/TOT. OPG. EXPENSE (R61)					3a		3a		8a	4a
TOT. SAL. + BENE./TOT. ASSETS (R63)				4b	9b	5b				
NET INCOME/TOT. EQUITY CAPITAL (R66)	3b				4b	4b	5b			
GROWTH IN TOT. CAPITAL ACCTS. (G76)							7a		6a	6a

Where the data contained in each cell indicates:

1 thru 9 = Relative importance of variable in each year based on the size of its standardized discriminant coefficient.
   a = Variable accounted for a significant change in the RAO V statistic at the .05 level.
   b = Variable accounted for a significant change in the RAO V statistic at the .10 level.

coefficient and the significance of the RAO V change revealed that this variable was not a strong discriminator relative to the others which entered and was only statistically significant at the .10 level. An analysis of the variable's group means indicates that the independent banks paid higher total compensation relative to total assets than did the affiliate banks for the first three years of the postacquisition period. This difference did continue throughout the later stages of the postacquisition period but was not statistically significant. This suggests that affiliate banks may have utilized a smaller percentage of human resources to conduct their operations than the independent banks. It is possible MBHCs may realize some economies of scale as it relates to the employment of human resources in their operations.

The investing policy performance dimension for this size category supported the results obtained in size category 2. It revealed that the investing policy of both groups did not display the differences that were identified with size category 1. It appears that although there are differences in this performance dimension it becomes less significant and appears less frequently the larger the relative size of the bank.

Size category 4. Since there were only 13 banks in this $51–100 million size category, the stepwise discriminant procedure produced a high level of instability. In several of the periods, the SDA could not be completed because of the small sample size. Therefore, the analysis of this size category was limited to an examination of the group means associated with each performance variable. No multivariate statistical testing could be conducted on this subset of banks.

Relative to investing policy, the independent banks did maintain a higher percentage of U.S. government securities to total assets than the affiliate banks. Since U.S. government securities are a major component of the other investing policy ratio highlighted in earlier SDA analyses (U.S. government securities + U.S. government agency securities + municipal securities/total deposits) this ratio reflected similar results. A noticeable difference in the group means appeared in the asset utilization ratios. An analysis of both the earning assets to total assets and earning assets to available funds ratios revealed that independent banks produced slightly higher percentages when compared to the affiliate banks. In each case the ratios tend to reflect consistently higher percentages for the independent banks immediately after acquisition. Since this is not consistent with the earlier results, it suggests that larger sized independent banks may outperform their affiliate counterparts. However, since no statistical testing could be conducted, no firm conclusion could be reached in this study.

The deposit structure, capital management, and asset composition ratios tended to follow the same pattern as earlier analyses. The only other significant difference appeared in the profitability ratio of net income to total equity capital. Whereas earlier analyses indicated very little profitability differences between the two, the group means compiled in this case indicated that these particular independent banks outperformed their affiliate bank counterparts in each year in both the pre-and postacquisition periods.

Size category 5. With only one set of affiliate and independent banks having an asset size greater than $100 million, the SDA analysis could not be applied. However, the performance variable's group means were computed and compared. The results of this comparison revealed that the financial performance profile of these two banks tended to track very closely with the results obtained in size category 4. The one independent bank did have higher asset utilization percentages and a greater profitability as measured by net income to total equity capital. Given that no significance testing could be conducted, the only conclusion that can be drawn is that the performance profiles as represented by the variable's group means are very similar to those in the $51–100 million size category. This suggests that there may not be much of a difference in financial performance between these two size categories.

Implications For Research Objectives

The empirical results obtained from the various multivariate analyses employed in this study offer some insight into the relative differences that existed between the performance profiles of affiliate and independent banks. The initial research objective was to determine if MBHC affiliation has a significant impact on the performance of a commercial bank. The results indicate that MBHC affiliation does appear to affect an affiliate bank's subsequent financial performance with respect to certain dimensions of performance. An analysis of both the pre- and postacquisition periods associated with a MBHC's acquisition of a commercial bank indicates that some differences in performance began to appear almost immediately after acquisition. As the time period after acquisition lengthens, the number of significant differences increases. Generally, by the end of the fifth year after acquisition nearly all of the performance differences have appeared. By the end of the postacquisition period both groups have begun to respond to competitive pressures, and in certain respects they begin to exhibit more similar performance profiles. The magnitude and the statistical significance of the performance differences that do consistently appear throughout the various stages of the postacquisition period strongly suggest that the null hypothesis that the performance of commercial banks is not significantly associated with MBHC affiliation be rejected. It appears that holding company affiliation does have some effect on a commercial bank's performance.

A second research objective was to determine which available performance measures best discriminate between affiliate and independent bank performance. An analysis of 310 banks suggests that there were at least 10 performance measures which discriminate between the two groups. A separate analysis of different size categories further highlighted other performance variables which did discriminate between affiliate and independent banks. In each case the results suggest that the null hypothesis that the centroids of the two groups of performance variables are equal must also be rejected. The statistical results associated with the multivariate analysis support the rejection of this hypothesis.

The third research objective was to determine over what time period any observed differences occur. The MDA classification results of Model 1 and the SDA results of Model 2 suggest that the length of the postacquisition period that is selected is a crucial factor in identifying the degree of difference that exists between the two groups of banks. The results imply that a postacquisition period of less than three years does not permit all the ultimate effects of MBHC affiliation to appear. In some cases it appears that it takes five years and longer for some aspects of holding company affiliation to have an effect on an acquired bank's financial performance. In short, the length of the postacquisition period used in a particular analysis appears to exert a strong influence on the ultimate results.

The final research objective was to identify what factors might be attributed to any performance differences and what public policy implications might be drawn from these results. The analysis of possible factors and their implications for public policy making is presented in chapter 5.

Summary

The results of the empirical analysis are presented and discussed in this chapter. Initially, selected performance variables of 155 banks which were acquired by MBHCs from 1968 to 1972 were compared to a control group of independent banks. The time period reviewed included a three-year preacquisition period and a five-year, and where possible six- to nine-year, postacquisition period. The analysis that followed was presented in the form of two models. The first model employed various data reduction techniques which were used ultimately to define a seven-factor multiple discriminant function. This discriminant function was able to explain approximately 78 percent of the total variance that existed in the data set. MDA classification procedures were conducted cross-sectionally over the pre- and postacquisition periods and over specific calendar year periods. These results indicated that the financial performance profiles of the two groups appeared to be affected by general economic conditions, monetary policy, and holding company affiliation. The analysis produced a 28 performance variable set that captured the basic performance differences of the two groups of banks. These variables were subsequently used as input data for Model 2.

Model 2 was designed to identify which of these performance variables accounted for the major performance differences between the two groups of banks. Specific dimensions of asset composition, asset utilization, investing policy, capital management, expense control, and profitability were identified as good discriminating variables. An analysis of the sign, relative strength, and statistical significance of these performance variables revealed that some specific changes in a performance profile do occur once a bank has been acquired by an MBHC. A subsequent analysis of the various size categories of banks suggested that these differences are generally consistent across each group. However, the results did indicate that the performance profiles associated with different sized matched pairs of affiliate and independent banks are somewhat different relative to specific dimensions of asset utilization, asset composition, and profitability.

5

Summary, Conclusions, and Recommendations for Further Research

Summary

The purpose of this study was to investigate empirically how well MBHC affiliate banks perform relative to their local independent bank counterparts. The main emphasis was on determining whether holding company affiliate banks perform any differently, once they have been acquired, from independent banks of comparable size operating under similar market conditions. More specifically, it attempted to determine whether or not holding company affiliation has any effect on commercial bank performance.

To evaluate the holding company effect on a recently acquired affiliate bank, an evaluation of the financial performance profiles of affiliate and independent banks was conducted. Prior research provided the foundation for this study. An attempt was made to overcome many of the limitations associated with previous studies. A multivariate research methodology was designed to analyze several different performance dimensions for a large number of commercial banks. Financial data were analyzed for a 14-year period, and the research design was structured to isolate as many external factors as possible.

A review of the literature relating the MBHC performance revealed that holding company affiliation does have some impact on bank performance. However, previous studies have not consistently agreed on either the magnitude and duration of these effects or on the specific financial performance dimensions which are impacted. In particular, the empirical results associated with a few multivariate studies did not confirm the results reported by numerous univariate studies. This study was aimed at developing a better understanding of the impact of holding company affiliation on the financial performance of a commercial bank.

The study was national in scope. It initially considered 76 performance variables. The universe of banks was drawn from all MBHC acquisitions that were acquired during the time period 1968–72, and these banks were examined over a time period considerably longer than most of the previous studies. Two multivariate models were designed to analyze any financial performance differences that might exist between two relatively large groups of affiliate and independent banks. Model 1 attempted to determine if MBHC affiliation had a significant impact on the performance of a commercial bank and, if so, over what time period any observed difference occurred. Model 2 was concerned with which available performance measures best discriminate between the two groups of banks.

This study is an extension of previous multivariate MBHC performance research. It extended and further defined the early work of Johnson and Meinster (Johnson and Meinster, 1975). It employed a cross-sectional analysis design and to that extent was similar to Mayne's attempt to use regression analysis to detect continuing performance differences between affiliate and independent banks (Mayne, 1977). However, this is the first study which attempts to use a multivariate methodology to address the joint issues of whether holding company affiliation affected a commercial bank's subsequent financial performance and, if so, over what time period.

To achieve the research objectives stated earlier in this study, several multivariate techniques were employed. Initially PCA was conducted to reduce the performance data to a new set of variables with as little loss of information as possible. Then additional data reduction techniques were employed to reduce the level of multicollinearity and to increase the percentage of explained total variance.

These techniques produced a seven-factor discriminant model which explained over 78 percent of the total variance in the data set. MDA classifications procedures conducted on a cross-sectional basis indicated that the performance profile of affiliate banks did change subsequent to their acquisition by various MBHCs. Since these performance differences appeared after acquisition, but not before, it was highly probable that the changes were, in part, due to the bank's affiliation with a holding company.

It was also determined that the performance differences which did appear did so in varying degrees throughout the postacquisition period. Some of the performance differences appeared almost immediately while others did not appear until several years after acquisition.

The postacquisition analysis also revealed another interesting aspect which is related to the joint effects of monetary policy and holding company affiliation on bank performance. Classification procedures performed on a calendar year basis revealed that tight monetary conditions did impact the performance of both affiliate and independent banks to such an extent that it neutralized some of the impact of the holding company affiliation.

SDA was conducted in an aggregate model on all banks in an attempt to identify which specific performance variables accounted for the observed performance differences. It was also conducted on groups of various size categories of banks to determine if both the larger and smaller sized affiliates tended to perform in a similar manner relative to their control groups.

Conclusions Resulting from the Study

The conclusions derived from this study are drawn directly from the empirical analysis set forth in chapter 4. These conclusions are based solely on those selected performance variables of the banks included in this study and reference only the specific time period tested. Any further generalization of the conclusions of this research must be done with considerable caution. The specific limitations of this study and their potential impact on these conclusions are discussed in a subsequent section of this final chapter.

MBHC Affiliation Impact

MBHC affiliation does have a measurable impact on the performance of a commercial bank. The discriminant model consistently revealed that affiliate banks do exhibit a different performance profile from their independent bank counterparts once they have been acquired. This was demonstrated by both the MDA classification and SDA results since these results revealed that affiliate banks had very similar performance profiles relative to their independent bank counterparts in the preacquisition period.

Time Dimension of Affiliation Impact

The performance differences that do exist between affiliate and independent banks began to appear almost immediately after a bank was acquired by an MBHC. Within three to five years after acquisition almost all performance differences were identified. The results indicate that the competitive factors operating in a bank's market area affect both affiliate and independent banks in such a way that most performance differences do not exist throughout the entire postacquisition period.

The most immediate impact of holding company affiliation appeared in the asset composition performance dimension. Specific performance differences in the deposit composition, operational efficiency, and capital management performance dimensions appeared later in the postacquisition period.

Performance Differences Identified

The affiliate bank group was characterized as having a higher level of asset utilization and a higher loan-to-deposit ratio when compared to the control group. Specifically, affiliate banks produced higher ratios of earning assets to total assets and of earning assets to available funds. They also had higher total loan to total deposit ratios.

Affiliate banks appeared to support their more aggressive asset acquisition, in part, by attracting longer term and more costly time deposits. This was highlighted by the higher total time deposit to total deposit ratios achieved by them.

They also operated with lower capital ratios as measured by the total capital account to total loan ratio. In the expense area, affiliate banks did produce higher expense ratios. In particular, they produced higher ratios of other operating expenses to total operating expenses.

Profitability Differences

Neither group of banks maintained a consistent profitability advantage relative to the other. The return on total assets measure of profitability failed to enter the stepwise discriminant function. While the return on equity profit measure did enter the stepwise discriminant function, it does so very inconsistently without a great deal of statistical strength or statistical significance. It appeared that whatever benefits accrued to the affiliate banks from a more aggressive asset portfolio were offset by higher other operating expenses and higher deposit costs.

Bank Size Differentials

The performance profile differences that resulted from the aggregate analysis were relatively uniform across all size categories tested. The most significant and most consistent difference among size categories appeared in the loan portfolio area. Smaller affiliate banks (less than $50 million) possessed higher ratios of consumer loans to total loans and of lower commercial and industrial loans to total loans than the control group. Larger independent banks (greater than $50 million) appeared to outperform affiliate banks in the asset utilization and profitability performance dimensions.

Throughout the entire analysis of various size categories there did not appear to be any performance differences that could be associated with any potential economies of scale advantage for the affiliate banks. Neither group was found to be operating with any sustained lower cost to total output type operating advantage.

Impact of Economic Conditions

Periods of tight monetary policy and the adverse economic conditions that accompany these periods also had a measurable impact on bank performance. MDA classification results revealed that the impact of holding company affiliation on bank performance was modified greatly by tight monetary conditions. Specifically, the tight monetary conditions that existed during the 1969–70 and 1973–75 time periods tended to neutralize any management or operating advantage associated with holding company affiliation. The results also suggested that the more restrictive the monetary policy was in any given time period the greater the relative impact it had on any performance differences that might exist.

Independent Bank Performance

The performance of independent banks also is modified by the appearance of a holding company affiliated bank. The MDA classification results indicate that independent banks do react to a holding company entry by, in time, taking on some of the characteristics of that affiliate as expressed by the discriminant function. This suggests that over time independent banks do react competitively to a holding company entrant in their marketplace. They do so to such an extent that they assume a performance profile designed to compete better with their new competition.

Contributions of the Study

The conclusions that are presented do provide some interesting extensions to the MBHC performance literature although not all the conclusions provide new evidence on this issue. The empirical results associated with this study offer an important extension of the MBHC performance literature. It is the first extensive multivariate analysis which attempts to address specifically the issue of the effect of holding company affiliation on bank performance. It used a large set of financial performance data to determine statistically which variables were the best discriminators between the two groups of banks rather than simply select certain variables for testing purposes. It examined a large universe of banks on a yearly basis over a three-year preacquisition period and a lengthy postacquisition period.

Confirmation of Previous Results

Viewing the conclusions individually, it is apparent that some of them are consistent with the results of earlier works while others tend to refute earlier findings. The results of the study confirmed the relatively consistent univariate finding that affiliated banks hold smaller ratios of U.S. government securities and devote a larger share of their deposits to loans as opposed to investments. It also confirmed the univariate findings that holding company banks have larger "other expenses" and that the profitability of a holding company affiliate is generally no better than, and in some cases worse than, independent banks of the same size.

A major contribution of this study relative to the univariate studies is that it does confirm certain univariate findings while overcoming the sampling procedure and multicollinearity differences noted by others (Johnson and Meinster, 1973, and Jessup, 1974).

The results of this study confirm some, but not all, of Mayne's multivariate findings. In particular her loan composition, capital management, and operating efficiency conclusions were generally confirmed (Mayne, 1977).

Refutation of Previous Results

Relative to the various univariate studies that had been previously conducted, the statistical results associated with the multivariate techniques did not reconfirm the univariate findings that affiliate banks hold substantially smaller ratios of cash assets and larger amounts of state and local government securities.

Relative to the other multivariate studies, the results do not confirm the Johnson and Meinster findings that the major difference between affiliate and independent banks was their pricing behavior. The results of the PCA conducted in this study are generally not consistent with those of Johnson and Meinster possibly because of the limited number of performance variables they used. However, these results do support their contention that the length of the postacquisition interval does have an effect on performance (Johnson and Meinster, 1975).

The results did not confirm Mayne's conclusion that an affiliate bank's profitability is greater than its independent bank counterparts. In fact, the results suggest that the larger sized independent banks may actually outperform their affiliate counterparts in the profitability area (Mayne, 1977).

New Evidence

By way of new evidence, this study reveals much more explicitly the interrelationship between the postacquisition interval selected and the performance profile differentials that result. Specifically, it revealed that a study which employed a relatively short postacquisition period (less than three years) would not capture those performance differences which appear to become evident after three years. In short, the results indicated that the relatively short postacquisition intervals employed by most univariate studies did not permit those studies to measure accurately any performance profile differences that might subsequently exist.

The study also revealed that the differences in performance that do exist may be influenced somewhat by the size of the banks involved. Specifically, the smaller affiliate banks demonstrated a significant preference for consumer lending relative to their independent counterparts. On the other hand, the smaller independent banks displayed a significant preference for making more commercial and industrial loans than their affiliate counterparts.

Limitations of the Analysis

The conclusions presented previously are based on the specific performance variables included in the analysis and the multivariate methodology used to test for the significance of those variables. The ability to generalize from these specific conclusions is therefore limited by the various assumptions and constraints inherent in this research design.

One particular assumption that underlies this research design is that the holding company segment of the commercial banking community is a relatively unique and homogeneous unit. To a great extent this assumption is true because commercial banks are heavily regulated institutions. However, the extent of the regulatory process may not carry over to the management structure of these organizations. If there is a great variation in the degree of centralization of managerial decisions or in any other managerial or behavioral characteristic, then any results based on the aggregate holding company sector cannot yield valid predictions about the behavior of any subset of MBHCs.

Even though this study contained a relatively large universe of banks, the utility of the study was limited by the fact that adequate matched pairs could generally be found only for banks that are considered to be relatively small (less than $50 million).

This was due to several factors. First, all "lead bank" acquisitions were removed from the analysis. Lead banks by their very nature are larger banks. This effectively limited the size of the affiliate banks included in the study. Secondly, the federal regulatory authorities essentially forced holding companies to purchase smaller banks through their enforcement of the nation's antitrust laws. Lastly, this situation resulted from an inability to pair up large affiliate banks with similar sized independent banks operating in the same market.

As a result, the stepwise discriminant analyses conducted on the three smallest size categories were able to produce statistically significant results since they contained approximately 90 percent of the total number of banks in the study. The stepwise discriminant analyses of the two largest size categories was severely restricted by the fact that only 14 matched pairs of banks were included in these categories. Therefore, an extension of the aggregate results must be limited primarily to smaller sized banks.

Since there were numerous changes to the Report of Condition and the Report of Income and Dividends during the period 1964–77, it was very difficult to construct ratios containing certain information because this information was not consistently collected over the 14-year period. As a result, some potential performance variables that appeared to be better measures of expense control and bank pricing could not be included in the analysis. This ultimately limited the overall ability of the discriminant model to identify discriminating variables that accurately reflect specific differences in certain performance dimensions that are best measured using income statement information.

Another limitation relates to the sampling technique. Most statistical analysis stipulates that random sampling be used in order that rigorous statistical inferences may be drawn from a sample about a population. The universe referred to in this study represents all possible affiliate banks for which the necessary data were available. The years 1968–72 were not selected at random but were chosen because of data availability from the Federal Reserve System and because MBHC acquisitions acquired much later would not have had a lengthy postacquisition interval for multivariate testing purposes. Hence, the multivariate statistical results of this study relate only to the subpopulation from which the universe of banks was selected.

Public Policy Implications

Federal legislation regulating bank holding companies has been enacted on three occasions in the past quarter of a century. As it has since 1933, the Congress of the United States consistently has placed the authority for reviewing and approving MBHC acquisitions with the Federal Reserve Board. Instead of restricting holding company development, these regulations have led to an increase in MBHC activities. This increase in activity has substantially changed the environment of commercial banking in the United States.

Even though the legal environment in recent years has created a condition conducive to the growth of MBHCs, this growth would not have occurred without specific economic incentives. Much of the literature relating to holding company performance suggests these reasons are more imaginary than real. On the other hand, many holding company proponents offer several economic arguments in justifying increased holding company activities.

The discussion of the legislation relative to bank holding companies in chapter 1 identified five factors that the Federal Reserve Board was to consider when evaluating a proposed acquisition of a bank. This study dealt with two of those factors. They were the earning prospects of the holding company and the bank concerned and the convenience and needs of the communities to be served. Therefore, to the extent that the results of this study shed new evidence on these factors, this study has specific public policy implications.

The central issue which our public policy makers continually face in their designated role as regulators of the bank holding company movement is whether or not the change in bank structure which results from the MBHC movement is in the public interest. They must be concerned whether or not any potential benefits of bank holding companies (lower costs of providing financial services) exceed their associated costs (greater concentration of resources) and therefore promote the general welfare of society. If MBHCs do affect the subsequent performance of commercial banks they acquire, are the differences which occur desirable? Do they foster greater competition, offer greater convenience, and adequately satisfy the banking needs of our society?

This study attempted to analyze a specific dimension that the Federal Reserve Board must consider before approving or disapproving an MBHC acquisition. This specific dimension was bank performance. Before any value judgments can be made on the implications of these results for the Federal Reserve Board, it is necessary to postulate what type of bank performance features might be in the public interest.

Commercial banks initially were created as a type of financial intermediary to provide two basic services. These two services were to accept deposits and to extend credit. As a financial institution, a commercial bank should perform these functions efficiently and economically. It must perform these duties in a safe and sound manner. Since a commercial bank must attempt to satisfy its customers' financial demands with a limited set of resources, it appears that it would be in the public interest if a commercial bank could satisfy a greater amount of its customers' credit demands at reasonable and prudent risk levels.

Operationally, these institutions should attempt to minimize their costs and offer a mix of financial services that is responsive to their customer's needs. Aside from any anticompetitive effects, the MBHC performance issue centers around whether or not the possible adverse consequences of some loss of local control of banks is more than offset by the greater public benefits that would arise from having a larger amount of bank credit made available to the economic units in the community.

The empirical results of this study indicate that affiliate banks do achieve higher earning asset utilization levels than comparable size independent banks. However, they do so with lower capital ratios and a higher ratio of other operating expenses to total operating expenses. They don't appear to be more profitable, nor do they appear to benefit from possible economies of scale that might exist in a holding company network. And smaller sized affiliate banks exhibited a preference for making more consumer loans than their comparable independent banks.

In light of these results and notwithstanding any anticompetitive problems that might be raised relative to MBHCs, it seems that on balance the performance effects of MBHCs generally do appear to be in the public interest. Affiliate banks appear to perform their credit and depository functions at least as well as, and in some cases better than, their independent bank counterparts. They appear to do so at reasonable risk levels without any negative effect to their income. Therefore, the Federal Reserve Board does appear to be fulfilling the legislative will of Congress to promote a banking structure that acts in the best interest of the public. The results of this study do not argue for any dramatic changes in the manner in which they exercise their supervisory and regulatory role in the MBHC area.

Public policy makers should also note that the MBHC impact on bank performance, although real and significant, is not as great as some economic arguments would contend. It is possible that part of the answer to this is that banks are generally subjected to market forces that cannot be altered simply through affiliation with a holding company unless the acquired bank is a very dominant bank in its market area. Since the Federal Reserve Board through its antitrust considerations does not approve the acquisition of dominant banks by holding companies, any performance changes tend to be limited by managerial initiative, economic conditions, and competition from other banks and financial institutions.

Recommendations for Further Research

Obviously the results of this study do not apply to all banks. The inability to generalize from these results was highlighted in an earlier portion of this chapter. Further research is necessary if a more complete understanding of the effect of MBHC affiliation on bank performance is to be achieved.

Further research is necessary on various size categories of banks to determine if the performance profile differentials exhibited in this study are truly uniform across all bank size categories. The structure of this study was limited by an inability to identify and then find a matched pair for larger affiliate banks. The number of years in which MBHCs acquired banks would have to be expanded to permit this type of research extension. Alternatively, univariate tests might be conducted on the limited number of large sized matched pairs and compared to similar test results for the smaller bank pairs.

Further research is also necessary in analyzing the MBHC performance impact in specific states which have very active and expansionary MBHCs. For example, an analysis of MBHC activity in Texas would isolate this issue of performance to a unique economic situation in a specific state and provide public policy makers with a better understanding of whether or not the public interest is being served in that particular state.

Another area of possible analysis would be a performance comparison between specific holding company systems and the larger branching networks of certain commercial banks. For example, this type of analysis could effectively contrast the performance of some large holding company systems in unit banking states like Texas and Colorado with specific branching networks organized in states like California.

A review of the literature relative to the MBHC performance controversy revealed that very little research had been conducted on the influence of different managerial philosophies or the impact of organization form on bank performance. Using the banks and the data identified in this study, additional research could be conducted to examine the impact of these issues on bank performance.

Finally, this type of multivariate methodology lends itself to ascertaining whether any financial institution performance differences do exist between two or more groups. For example, this research methodology could be applied to examining the performance effect related to a conversion from a mutual type savings and loan association to a stock association. Thrift institution public policy makers are extremely interested in this issue as a result of the recent rush of savings and loan associations to convert from a mutual to a stock form of association.

Notes

Chapter 1

1. The study does not consider all bank holding companies. The primary reason is that the formation of OBHCs does not, per se, alter market and state structure, but MBHC expansion, by definition, changes banking structure.

2. Bank holding companies are usually separately chartered corporations, but a bank which owns stock in one or more other banks may itself be a bank holding company.

3. A unit bank is a single office institution where all official banking services are offered.

4. *Annual Statistical Digest*, Board of Governors of the Federal Reserve System, 1973–77.

5. *The Federal Reserve System: Functions and Purposes*, 1974.

6. The act defined holding companies in such a way that OBHCs were exempt from the act.

7. A *de novo* bank is a newly chartered bank or branch.

8. *The Federal Reserve System: Functions and Purposes*, 1974.

Chapter 2

1. All future references to bank holding companies shall be considered synonymous with MBHCs unless otherwise stated.

2. Multivariate methods are a collection of procedures for analyzing associations between two or more sets of measurements that have been made on each object in one or more samples of objects.

3. The banking data referred to were the various performance measures commonly computed from the Report of Condition and Report of Income.

Chapter 3

1. The term independent bank commonly is used to refer to a bank that is not affiliated with any MBHC. It does not have any reference to any particular political or trade organization.

2. Market area designations were obtained from the FDIC's annual publication, *Bank Operating Statistics*.

3. For example, loan to deposit ratios and deposit mix were examined to match banks with similar sources and uses of funds.

4. Whenever possible, member affiliate banks were matched with member independent banks and nonmember affiliate banks were matched with nonmember independent banks.

5. The lists of *de novo* acquisitions and those acquisitions involving OBHCs were obtained from the Federal Reserve Board of Governors.

6. Some ratios included in this group measure basically the same performance dimension. However, subsequent steps in the research design select the one measure of that performance dimension which best discriminates between the two groups of banks.

7. The five distinct sets of banks used in this study are identified by the years in which the banks were acquired. For example, banks acquired in 1968 are treated as one distinct set of banks, banks acquired in 1969 as another distinct set, through banks acquired in 1972.

8. For a more detailed discussion of the required scaling properties of data used in various multivariate techniques, see Fred N. Kerlinger, *Foundations of Behavioral Research*, Holt Rinehart and Winston, Inc., second edition, 1974, chapter 3.

9. R. J. Rummel, "Understanding Factor Analysis," *Journal of Conflict Resolution* (1968), pp. 443–80.

10. Paul Green, *Analyzing Multivariate Data*, 1978, The Dryden Press, Hinsdale, Illinois.

Chapter 4

1. Several stepwise selection criteria were analyzed in the SDA analysis. The RAO V statistic is a generalized distance measure and is offered by many statisticians as a useful selection criteria because the change in V has a chi-square distribution with one degree of freedom. Therefore, it can be tested for statistical significance.

Bibliography

Periodicals

Baltensperger, Ernst, "Cost of Banking Activities: Interactions Between Risk and Operating Costs," *Journal of Money, Credit, and Banking* (August, 1972), pp. 595–611.
———, "Economies of Scale, Firm Size, and Concentration in Banking," *Journal of Money, Credit, and Banking* (August, 1972), pp. 467–88.
Benston, George G., "Economies of Scale of Financial Institutions," *Journal of Money, Credit, and Banking* (May, 1972), pp. 312–41.
———, "The Optimal Banking Structure: Theory and Evidence," *Journal of Bank Research* (Winter, 1973), pp. 220–37.
Boczar, Gregory E., "The Determinants of Multibank Holding Company Formations," *Southern Economic Journal* (July, 1975), pp. 120–29.
———, "Market Characteristics and Multibank Holding Company Acquisitions," *Journal of Finance* (March, 1977), pp. 131–46.
Bowsher, Norman N., "Have Multibank Holding Companies Affected Commercial Bank Performance," *Business Review*, Federal Reserve Bank of St. Louis (April, 1978), pp. 8–15.
Burke, Jim, "Bank Holding Company Behavior and Structural Change," *Journal of Bank Research* (Spring, 1978), pp. 43–51.
Chase, Samuel B., and John J. Mingo, "The Regulation of Bank Holding Companies," *Journal of Finance* (May, 1975), pp. 281–92.
Cohen, Kalman J., and Samuel Reid, "Effects of Regulation, Branching, and Mergers on Banking Structure and Performance," *Southern Economic Journal* (October, 1967), pp. 231–49.
Crosse, Howard, "Banking Structure and Competition," *Journal of Finance* (May, 1965), pp. 349–57.
Daniel, Donnie L., William A. Longbrake, and Neil B. Murphy, "The Effect of Technology on Bank Economies of Scale for Demand Deposits," *Journal of Finance* (March, 1973), pp. 131–46.
Darnell, Jerome C., "Determinants of Chain Banking," *National Banking Review* (June, 1967), pp. 459–68.
———, "Performance Characteristics of Banks Acquired by Colorado Holding Companies," *Bank News* (November, 1977), pp. 9–16, 40–42.
Drum, Dale S., "MBHCs: Evidence After Two Decades of Regulations," *Business Conditions*, Federal Reserve Bank of Chicago (December, 1976), pp. 3–15.
Fischer, Gerald C., "Bank Holding Company Affiliates: Branches or Unit Banks," *Journal of Business* (January, 1964), pp. 47–49.

Francis, Darryl R., "Economic Forces Facing the Bank Holding Company Movement," *Monthly Review*, Federal Reserve Bank of St. Louis (September, 1974), pp. 8–12.

Fraser, Donald R., and Peter S. Rose, "The Impact of Holding Company Acquisitions on Bank Performance," *Bankers Magazine* (Spring, 1973), pp. 47–61.

————, "More on Banking Structure: The Evidence from Texas," *Journal of Financial and Quantitative Analysis* (January, 1971), pp. 601–11.

Fraser, Donald R., Wallace J. Phillips, and Peter S. Rose, "A Canonical Analysis of Bank Performance," *Journal of Financial and Quantitative Analysis* (March, 1974), pp. 287–95.

Gallick, Edward C., "Bank Profitability and Bank Size," *Monthly Review*, Federal Reserve Bank of Kansas City (January, 1976), pp. 11–16.

Goldberg, Lawrence G., "Bank Holding Company Acquisitions and Their Impact on Market Shares," *Journal of Money, Credit, and Banking* (February, 1976), pp. 127–30.

Greenbaum, Stuart L., "Competition and Efficiency in the Banking System—Empirical Research and Its Policy Implications," *Journal of Political Economy* (August, 1967), pp. 461–73.

Heggestad, Arnold A., "Riskiness of Investments in Nonbank Activities by Bank Holding Companies," *Journal of Economics and Business* (Spring, 1975), pp. 219–23.

Heggestad, Arnold A., and John J. Mingo, "Capital Management by Holding Company Banks," *Journal of Business* (October, 1975), pp. 500–05.

————, "Prices, Nonprices, and Concentration in Commercial Banking," *Journal of Money, Credit, and Banking* (February, 1976), pp. 107–17.

Herzig-Marx, Chayim, "Holding Companies and Deposit Variability," *Business Conditions*, Federal Reserve Bank of Chicago (March, 1976), pp. 12–15.

Hobson, Hugh A., John T. Masten, and Jacobus T. Severiens, "Holding Company Acquisitions and Bank Performance: A Comparative Study," *Journal of Bank Research* (Summer, 1978), pp. 116–20.

Hoffman, Stuart, "A Florida Case Study: Performance of Holding Company Banks," *Monthly Review*, Federal Reserve Bank of Atlanta (December, 1975), pp. 16–23.

Holland, Robert C., "Bank Holding Companies and Financial Stability," *Journal of Financial and Quantitative Analysis* (November, 1975), pp. 577–87.

Jessee, Michael A., and Steven A. Seelig, "An Analysis of the Public Benefits Test of the Bank Holding Company Act," *Monthly Review*, Federal Reserve Bank of New York (June, 1974), pp. 151–62.

Jessup, Paul F., "Analyzing Acquisitions by Bank Holding Companies," *Journal of Bank Research* (Spring, 1973), pp. 55–63.

Johnson, Rodney D., and David R. Meinster, "An Analysis of Bank Holding Company Acquisitions: Some Methodological Issues," *Journal of Bank Research* (Spring, 1973), pp. 58–61.

————, "The Performance of Bank Holding Company Acquisitions: A Multivariate Analysis," *Journal of Business* (April, 1975), pp. 204–12.

Kaufman, George G., "Bank Market Structure and Performance: The Evidence From Iowa," *Southern Economic Journal* (April, 1966), pp. 429–39.

Lawrence, Robert J., and Samuel H. Talley, "An Assessment of Bank Holding Companies," *Federal Reserve Bulletin* (January, 1973), pp. 15–21.

Light, Jack S., "Effects of Holding Company Affiliation on De Novo Banks," *Business Conditions*, Federal Reserve Bank of Chicago (July, 1976), pp. 11–15.

Mayne, Lucille S., "A Comparative Study of Bank Holding Company Affiliates and Independent Banks, 1969–1972," *Journal of Finance* (March, 1977), pp. 147–58.

————, "Management Policies of Bank Holding Companies and Bank Performance," *Journal of Bank Research* (Spring, 1976), pp. 37–48.

McLeary, Joe W., "Absentee Ownership—Its Impact on Bank Holding Company Performance," *Monthly Review*, Federal Reserve Bank of Atlanta (August, 1969), pp. 99–101.

———, "Bank Holding Companies: Their Growth and Performance," *Monthly Review*, Federal Reserve Bank of Atlanta (October, 1968), pp. 131–38.

Mingo, John J., "Capital Management and Profitability of Prospective Holding Company Banks," *Journal of Financial and Quantitative Analysis* (June, 1975), pp. 191–203.

———, "Managerial Motives, Market Structure, and the Performance of Holding Company Banks," *Economic Inquiry* (September, 1976), pp. 411–24.

Mote, Larry R., "The Perennial Issue: Branch Banking," *Business Conditions*, Federal Reserve Bank of Chicago (February, 1974), pp. 1–23.

Moyer, R. Charles, and Edward Sussna, "Registered Bank Holding Company Acquisitions: A Cross Section Analysis," *Journal of Financial and Quantitative Analysis* (September, 1973), pp. 647–61.

Murphy, Neil B., "Cost of Banking Activities: Interactions Between Risk and Operating Costs: A Comment," *Journal of Money, Credit, and Banking* (August, 1972), pp. 614–15.

Piper, Thomas R., and Steven J. Weiss, "The Profitability of Bank Acquisitions by Multibank Holding Companies," *New England Economic Review* (September/October, 1971), pp. 2–12.

———, "The Profitability of Multibank Holding Company Acquisitions," *Journal of Finance* (March, 1974), pp. 163–74.

Rose, Peter S., and Donald R. Fraser, "The Impact of Holding Company Acquisitions on Bank Performance," *Bankers Magazine* (Spring, 1973), pp. 85–91.

Rosenblum, Harvey, "Bank Holding Companies: An Overview," *Business Conditions*, Federal Reserve Bank of Chicago (August, 1973), pp. 3–13.

———, "Bank Holding Company Review—Part I," *Business Conditions*, Federal Reserve Bank of Chicago (February, 1975), pp. 3–10.

———, "Bank Holding Companies—Part II," *Business Conditions*, Federal Reserve Bank of Chicago (April, 1975), pp. 13–15.

Schweitzer, Stuart A., "Economies of Scale and Holding Company Affiliation in Banking," *Southern Economic Journal* (October, 1972), pp. 258–66.

Silverberg, Stanley C., "Bank Holding Companies and Capital Adequacy," *Journal of Bank Research* (Autumn, 1975), pp. 202–07.

Smith, Tynan, "Research on Banking Structure and Performance," *Federal Reserve Bulletin* (April, 1966), pp. 488–98.

Snider, Thomas E., "The Effect of Merger on the Lending Behavior of Rural Banks in Virginia," *Journal of Bank Research* (Spring, 1973), pp. 52–57.

Talley, Samuel H., "Bank Holding Company Operations and Performance," *The Magazine of Bank Administration* (October, 1973), pp. 26–29.

Varvel, Walter A., "A Valuation Approach to Bank Holding Company Acquisitions," *Economic Review*, Federal Reserve Bank of Richmond (July/August, 1975), pp. 9–15.

Ware, Robert F., "Banking Structure and Performance: Some Evidence From Ohio," *Economic Review*, Federal Reserve Bank of Cleveland (March, 1972), pp. 3–14.

———, "The Changing Structure of Bank Holding Companies," *Economic Review*, Federal Reserve Bank of Cleveland (April, 1969), pp. 3–11.

———, "Performance of Banks Acquired by Multibank Holding Companies in Ohio," *Economic Review*, Federal Reserve Bank of Cleveland (March/April, 1973), pp. 19–22.

Weiss, Steven J., "Bank Holding Companies and Public Policy," *New England Economic Review*, Federal Reserve Bank of Boston (January/February, 1969), pp. 3–27.

———, "Factors Affecting Bank Structure Change: The New England Experience,

1963–1974," *The New England Economic Review*, Federal Reserve Bank of Boston (July/August, 1975), pp. 16–25.

Whitehead, David D., and B. Frank King, "Multibank Holding Companies and Local Market Concentration," *Monthly Review*, Federal Reserve Bank of Atlanta (April, 1976), pp. 34–43.

Yeats, Alexander J., "Further Evidence on the Structure-Performance Relationship in Banking," *Journal of Economics and Business* (Winter, 1974), pp. 95–100.

Books, Proceedings, Working Papers, and Other Sources

Association of Registered Bank Holding Companies, *The Bank Holding Company: Its History and Significance in Modern America* July, 1973.

Bell, Frederick W., and Neil B. Murphy, *Costs in Commercial Banking: A Quantitative Analysis of Bank Behavior and Its Relation to Bank Regulation*, Research Report No. 41, Federal Reserve Bank of Boston, 1968.

Boczar, Gregory E., *The Growth of Multibank Holding Companies: 1965–1973*, Staff Economic Study No. 85, Board of Governors of the Federal Reserve System, 1975.

Boxman, Edith S., *Bank Holding Company Trends in New England*, Federal Reserve Bank of Boston, March, 1974.

Crosse, Howard D., and George Hempel, *Management Policies for Commercial Banks*, Englewood Cliffs, N.J., Prentice-Hall, Inc., 1973.

Federal Laws Regulating Bank Mergers and the Acquisition of Banks by Registered Bank Holding Companies, Federal Reserve Bank of Cleveland, 1971.

The Federal Reserve System: Purposes and Functions, Board of Governors of the Federal Reserve System, Washington, D.C., 1974.

Fischer, Gerald C., *American Banking Structure*, Columbia University Press, New York, 1968.

Fischer, Gerald C., *Banking Holding Companies*, Columbia University Press, New York, 1961.

Fraas, Arthur G., *The Performance of Individual Bank Holding Companies*, Staff Economic Study No. 84, Board of Governors of the Federal Reserve System, June, 1974.

Graddy, Duane B., *The Bank Holding Company Performance Controversy*, University Press of America, Washington, D.C., 1979.

Gup, Benton E., *Financial Intermediaries: An Introduction*, Boston, Massachusetts, Houghton Mifflin Company, 1976.

Heggestad, Arnold A., "Market Structure, Risk, and Profitability in the Banking Industry," *Proceedings of a Conference on Bank Structure and Competition*, Federal Reserve Bank of Chicago, 1972.

Hoffman, Stuart, *The Impact of Holding Company Affiliation on Bank Performance: A Case Study of Two Florida Multibank Holding Companies*, Working Paper Series, Federal Reserve Bank of Atlanta, January, 1976.

Jackson, William, "Commercial Banking Performance Sources: A Multivariate Model," *Proceedings on Bank Structure and Competition*, Federal Reserve Bank of Chicago, 1975.

Jessup, Paul F., "Acquisition by Bank Holding Companies: Promise, Performance, and Potential," *Proceedings of a Conference on Bank Structure and Competition*, Federal Reserve Bank of Chicago, 1974.

Lawrence, Robert J., *The Performance of Bank Holding Companies*, Board of Governors of the Federal Reserve System, June, 1967.

————, *Operating Policies of Bank Holding Companies*, Staff Economic Study No. 59, Board of Governors of the Federal Reserve System, March, 1971.

———, *Operating Policies of Bank Holding Companies*, Staff Economic Study No. 81, Board of Governors of the Federal Reserve System, 1974.

Office of the Comptroller of the Currency, *Studies in Banking Competition and the Banking Structure*, January, 1966.

Piper, Thomas R., *The Economics of Bank Acquisitions by Registered Bank Holding Companies*, Research Report No. 48, Federal Reserve Bank of Boston, March, 1971.

Talley, Samuel H., "Developments in the Bank Holding Company Movement," *Proceedings of a Conference on Bank Structure and Competition*, Federal Reserve Bank of Chicago, 1971.

Talley, Samuel H., *The Effect of Holding Company Acquisitions on Bank Performance*, Staff Economic Study No. 69, Board of Governors of Federal Reserve System, 1974.

———, *The Impact of Holding Company Acquisitions on Aggregate Concentration in Banking*, Staff Economic Report No. 80, Board of Governors of the Federal Reserve System, Spring, 1974.

Multivariate Analysis and Statistical Testing References

Altman, Edward I., "Financial Ratios, Discriminant Analysis, and the Prediction of Corporate Bankruptcy," *Journal of Finance* (September, 1968), pp. 589–609.

Dince, Robert R., and James C. Fortson, "The Use of Discriminant Analysis to Predict the Capital Adequacy of Commercial Banks," *Journal of Bank Research* (Spring, 1972), pp. 54–62.

Eisenbeis, Robert A., *Discriminant Analysis: Application, Potential, and Pitfalls*, FDIC Working Paper 75-2.

———, "Pitfalls in the Application of Discriminant Analysis in Business, Finance, and Economics," *Journal of Finance* (June, 1977), pp. 875–99.

Green, Paul E., *Analyzing Multivariate Data*, Hinsdale, Illinois, Dryden Press, 1978.

Joy, O. Maurice, and John O. Tollefson, "On the Financial Applications of Discriminant Analysis," *Journal of Financial and Quantitative Analysis* (December, 1975), pp. 723–39.

———, "Some Clarifying Comments on Discriminant Analysis," *Journal of Financial and Quantitative Analysis* (March, 1978), pp. 197–200.

Klemkosky, Robert C., and J. William Petty, "A Multivariate Analysis of Stock Price Variability," *Journal of Business Research* (Summer, 1973), pp. 1–10.

Kerlinger, Fred N., *Foundations of Behavioral Research*, New York, N.Y., Holt Reinhardt and Winston, Inc., 1973.

Lachenbrunch, Peter A., and M. Ray Mickey, "Estimation of Error Rates in Discriminant Analysis," *Technometrics* (February, 1978), pp. 1–11.

Neter, John, and William Wasserman, *Applied Linear Statistical Models*, Homewood, Illinois, Richard D. Irwin, Inc., 1974.

Pinches, George E., and Kent A. Mingo, "A Multivariate Analysis of Industrial Bond Ratings," *Journal of Finance* (March, 1973), pp. 1–15.

Ricketts, Donald, and Roger Stover, "An Examination of Commercial Bank Financial Ratios," *Journal of Bank Research* (Summer, 1978), pp. 121–24.

Rummel, R. J., "Understanding Factor Analysis," *Journal of Conflict Resolution* (1968), pp. 443–80.

Saunders, Robert J., "On the Interpretation of Models Explaining Cross-Sectional Differences among Commercial Banks," *Journal of Financial and Quantitative Analysis* (March, 1969), pp. 25–35.

Senter, R. J., *Analysis of Data*, Glenview, Illinois, Scott, Foresman and Company, 1969.

Winkler, Robert L., and William L. Hays, *Statistics: Probability, Inference, and Decision*, New York, N.Y., Holt, Reinhardt, and Winston, 1971.

Index